THE WILL TO CHANGE

ABOUT THE AUTHOR

As an instinctive philosopher and entrepreneur, J.T. Sullivan has long had a personal interest in the nature of human endeavour and the search for happiness and self-fulfilment. A proven marathon runner, his own business ventures include a successful dental clinic and home for the elderly. He is also highly regarded as an after-dinner speaker and more recently became a local councillor. He is currently working on the next volume in his 'Will to' series.

– From stress to success –

THE WILL TO CHANGE

OPTIONS FOR SUCCESS THROUGHOUT LIFE

J.T. SULLIVAN

RENAISSANCE BOOKS

THE WILL TO CHANGE
Options for success throughout life

First published 1995 by Renaissance Books Ltd
PO Box 219, Folkestone
Kent CT20 3LZ, England

© 1995 J.T. Sullivan

ISBN 1-898823-25-1 (paperback)

All rights reserved. No part of this publication
may be reproduced or transmitted in any form or by
any means without prior permission in writing
from the Publishers.

British Library Cataloguing in Publication Data
A CIP catalogue entry for this book is available
from the British Library

Set in Futura 12pt by Bookman, Slough, Berkshire
Printed and bound in England by Cromwell Press Ltd,
Melksham, Wiltshire

To Elizabeth
My strength where I am weak.

Also to Dermot, Niamh and Niall

Music to Remember

While writing this book, music played an important and inspirational part in assisting the free flow of ideas and the will to succeed. I offer my selection to readers as something to consider in their own quest:

* The music of Jean-Baptiste Lully – hauntingly beautiful
* Mendelssohn's piano concertos 1 and 2 – most relaxing and beautiful
* Six concerti grossi by Corelli – each one a joy
* The music of Vivaldi – always something to enjoy
* All the violin concertos, but especially Brahms – and especially the second movement
* The music of Mozart, particularly the concerto for Flute & Harp (K299) and especially the Requiem. The Lacrimosa is a special piece. So is the Ave Verum, in particular the Vespere salennes de confessore (K339) sung by Maria Zadori
* The music of Beethoven – especially his piano music.

CONTENTS

Foreword — xi
Acknowledgements — xiii
Introduction — xv

1. You already make changes to change how you feel — 1
2. The most common way people try to change is through diet — 1
3. What kind of person are you? — 2
4. Do you want to change? — 3
5. Most 'excess luggage' is manifested as stress — 5
6. On the source of stress — 7
7. The damage of stress — 9
8. On depression — 10
9. Who do you talk to most each day? — 11
10. Why you feel the way you do today? — 12
11. When you decide to change — 13
12. Write your own CV — 14
13. On visualizing change — 15
14. On quality — 16
15. So, where do you start? — 18
16. The first step in relaxing — 19
17. Meditation and family life — 20
18. On making decisions — 24
19. Understanding blame; understanding 'You Plc' — 25
20. Dealing with problems — 26
21. How do you maintain your body (your Plc)? — 27
22. How are you packaged? What sort of product are you? — 28
23. Feeding body and mind — 29
24. On preparing for everything in life — 30
25. Responsibility to a new-born baby — 32

26. On childhood	33
27. On re-birth	34
28. On self-consciousness	35
29. On first impressions	36
30. On role-play	36
31. On dress	37
32. On understanding the problems of others	39
33. On body language	40
34. On the new you	42
35. On inferiority	43
36. On being civilized	43
37. More on the new you	46
38. The mind and psychogenic illness	47
39. On pain	48
40. On the need for being fit	49
41. On being human	51
42. On being intelligent	52
43. What are emotions?	52
44. On acting	56
45. Free will	57
46. Mental cocoon, mental barriers and the 'comfort zone'	58
47. Think positive, not negative	59
48. On competing	60
49. Something about our IQ	61
50. On becoming adult	63
51. On being human	64
52. Goals for achieving happiness	65
53. On running	67
54. Running lessons for life	70
55. Peace of mind	72
56. On success	73
57. On nourishing the mind	74
58. On trying to impress	75
59. On individual qualities	76
60. On bravery	77
61. On exploring our potential	78
62. Expressing emotions	80

63. On relaxation and visualization	80
64. On self-expression	82
65. The principle of communication	83
66. More reflections on self-talk and control of our thoughts	85
67. Personal space and 'the clearing of the jungle'	87
68. The survival instinct	88
69. On giving yourself credit	89
70. On setting limits on ourselves	90
71. On giving	91
72. On our individuality	93
73. The right to succeed	94
74. On the fear of failure	94
75. On the past	95
76. On dealing with others	96
77. On embracing the whole world	98
78. On our spirituality	99
79. We are not alone	100
80. On dreams	100
81. The journey to work	102
82. Who are you?	104
83. On judging others	105
84. On others judging us	106
85. On thought and the subconscious	106
86. How the mind works	108
87. The power of thought	109
88. Discovering our excellence	110
89. On morning activity	111
90. On moods and happiness	112
91. On humour	113
92. On making meetings worthwhile	114
93. On the need for self-analysis	116
94. On making better decisions	117
95. On guilt and blame	124
96. On responsibility	126
97. On dealing with worry	128
98. On the forces within and without	129
99. How the body is affected chemically by our surroundings	130

100. On awareness	131
101. On body rhythms and control	132
102. On how to find happiness	135
103. On travelling through life with conviction	136
104. Twelve ways to improve the functions of the mind	138
105. The end and the beginning	139

FOREWORD

Most people live with an unhealthy level of stress and anxiety only ever dreaming of being happy or of success.

Have you ever wished that you could start life over again with all that you know now?

Supposing that just this very minute you had the most extraordinary experience and were born. You discover that everything up to now was just a training-ground for life. The more you have experienced in this training the more knowledge you have, all of which is stored in your subconscious. Unfortunately, there were some bad trainers and the unhappy bits, the flawed bits of your training, seemed to take precedence in expression over the good bits. But there would be no point in being born again if you did not have experience. There would be no greater opportunity in life a second time round. Your past is your wisdom. Your past experiences – good and bad – are very valuable things, most certainly not things that should paralyse you in any way.

People who want to start over again wish to do so because of their present state of mind. They are paralysed by their past. This is experienced as stress, anxiety, fear, and general unhappiness as well as lack of success or achievement. Your body is controlled by hormones every minute of the day, your emotions are how you feel as these hormones affect your body. Stress and happiness are how you feel under very different cocktails of hormones.

To move from stress to happiness to achievement and success, you need to understand the subconscious mind and how it has been programmed. You need also to understand your dreams and your nightmares, and then to gain an understanding of the chemistry of the brain. That is, the chemistry of emotion, of memory and of thought.

You need to look also at the external forces that act upon you, particularly upon your subconscious mind. Only then can we look at how it is possible to use the body's own chemistry to change the way you feel and to plan how to achieve success. The fact of the matter is that you *can* achieve your wildest dreams by applying the simplest of techniques for controlling your own mind.

The book will be best used by a relaxed and quick read through. Then by re-reading slowly, hopefully many times. It is intended as a guided tour through the psychology of the pursuit of success, excellence and self-confidence. It is a journey to happiness. It is a treasure hunt.

We will visit many important landmarks where we will find clues to the treasure. The ultimate clue will tell you who you are, and having found that you will have found the treasure; a whole treasure-chest of happiness and freedom and all that goes with it. You will have discovered self-confidence and the ability of self-expression.

A recurring message in the early part of the book is do not *try* to change. You just simply have to have the *desire* for change and change will come. Read casually at first and re-read; the more often you read the more you will find.

J.T.S.
Spring 1995

ACKNOWLEDGEMENTS

A few years ago at a time of high motivation and some achievement in my life I heard a taped series by Brian Tracey called the 'Psychology of Achievement'. There was nothing new in this series but it struck a chord with me which motivated me much further. I then heard a series from Wayne Dyer called 'The Universe Within', which counter-balanced the drive for achievement through constant goal-setting with a relaxing approach to the pursuit of happiness. Very recently, I heard an intriguing series by Deepak Chopra called 'Ageless Body – Timeless Mind' which gave great meaning to what I had written.

A manuscript such as this is a very personal thing so it was with much anxiety that I approached publishers. I need not have been anxious. I was fortunate to meet Paul Norbury. I am most grateful to him for his belief in and support for what I was trying to achieve. He is an artist with the written word who skillfully crafted mine. My thanks also to Geoffrey Murray whose incisive comments were so valuable, and a particular thanks to Vanessa Hooton my secretary for many late hours.

Introduction
THE WILL TO CHANGE

We all have past-times and hobbies which give us great satisfaction and in most cases we constantly try to improve at them.

I would like you to take an analogy of a golfer as substitute for your own pet pursuit.

If you were on a golf course and someone came up to you and said: 'Excuse me, but I have been watching you and I feel I can offer some advice on how to improve your swing.'

Would you react gratefully and with excitement at the prospect of improving your game, or would you react angrily saying: 'I have been swinging this club my way for twenty years and I am not about to change?'

Having taken the free lesson you go to the car-park and spend some time manoeuvering your car from a difficult parking spot. Someone comes and taps on your window and says: 'I have been watching you and I think I can offer some help in improving your car-manoeuvering skills.' How do you react now?

While you are out of your car dealing with this objectionable person someone comes up to you and taps you on the shoulder and says: 'I have been watching you and you seem to have a problem with stress in your life. I think I can improve your quality of life.' How would you react now?

Just to stretch the analogy a little further, supposing that in the crowd gathering to watch this very public row is your fairy godmother and she, like all good fairy godmothers, offers you three wishes. What would you choose? The first might be to get off a murder charge, the second might very well be for peace of mind. Who is there that gives the same attention to their state of mind as they do to their golf swing or their pet pursuit?

But we all know there is no fairy godmother. Or is there? Your fairy godmother is in your mind.

All you have to do is wish.

Read on and all will become clear if you have the will to change.

1. You already make changes to change how you feel

Would you go to an important engagement, social or otherwise, without dressing suitably, and attending to your hair? Before entering the meeting or the group, would you look in the mirror to see how you looked? If you found something amiss would you change it? If you did not do that how would you feel?

Even with this simple example, you can see that by changing the way you think, you can change the way you feel and that your mind has the power to produce dramatic physiological changes in your body.

You must accept also that you can re-programme your mind to rid yourself of all those parts of the old that give you negative and restricting moods. Because the way in which you learned any habit, indeed anything you do in life is by repetition over and over again until it was ingrained in your mind. You can, therefore, change any habit and form new ones by the same repetition.

2. The most common way people try to change is through dieting

I can recommend a good diet. A bowl of good muesli with skimmed milk three times a day for a month and you will lose weight, and you will not be too hungry and hopefully you will not damage your health.

Ah, you say, I cannot stand the stuff. I hate nuts – I cannot stand dried bananas. I think skimmed milk is awful.

Herein lies the problem. There are probably as many diets as there are people in the world. They all start tomorrow or next Monday and we can all find plenty of reasons why any particular diet is not the one for us.

There is obviously the need for a good diet otherwise so many people would not try or at least talk about trying, but before we can know the ultimate diet which is to be found in the pages of this book, we must look at the reasons for dieting.

That is too easy, you say, the reasons are obvious – Health, Fitness, Looking Good. But what do these add up to? The answer is simple – it is SELF IMAGE – that is the way you see yourself the way you feel about yourself. You can go on a crash diet, lose a lot of weight, but not change the person within and in most cases the weight just comes back again.

3   What kind of person are you?

How do you feel about yourself?

How do you feel in company?
What do you think others think of you?
Are you fit and healthy?

What do you think about when you lie awake at four o'clock in the morning?

What made you this way?

4 | Do you want to change?

This book is a guide to working out why you are the way you are and shows you ways to change the way you think and the way you see yourself.

There are those who will argue that you are the way you are because you were born that way, that your destiny is genetic and that you cannot change it. While there are undoubtedly certain genetic limitations on our ability, most of the way you are is moulded by experiences which have programmed you that way.

You can change the programming. You can learn new ways and by buying this book you have already indicated to yourself that you have the desire to do so.

If you doubt the power of your subconscious mind just stop and think for one moment.

Have you ever had a very bad nightmare? You are being chased by a lunatic with a knife or a vicious wild animal. You are running as fast as you can but it is not fast enough and you cannot find the way out. You awaken screaming and sweating and breathless.

It was all a dream and yet you are in this state. Your mind did this. Why you had this dream we will discuss later. Your mind can bring on all the results of great exertion while you sleep.

Now close your eyes again and imagine you are in a beautiful garden. You are sitting by a stream basking in the warm sunshine, the only sound is the buzzing of bees in the flowers and the water trickling over the rocks. You are at peace. Now imagine you turn a corner and there, before you, is a body grotesquely wounded by an attacker, with blood everywhere. Now how do you feel? From being very peaceful you are suddenly feeling sick and scared. How did that happen?

By the power of your mind in seconds you have changed your mood simply by using your imagination. What is demonstrated here is the power of learned reactions to experiences. This programming is stored in your subconscious and controls your existence unless you take control with your conscious mind.

To be fully in conscious control you need to be aware of all outside forces and the forces from within. This statement will be clarified as you read through the book, but for now you must just be aware of the difference between the two types of control of the body.

All diets that I have seen are about depriving oneself of food to change physical shape. The best diet will feed the mind and change the way you feel about yourself so that you will be motivated and positive and not need all those useless foods which damage your body. In short, instead of depriving yourself you will simply be doing what you want.

So this book should be seen as a diet for and from the mind and instead of weighing in, you must measure the weight of excess luggage you are carrying around your head. That excess luggage is guilt, worry, anger, frustration, loneliness, inferiority as well as all that is negative. These must be changed for positive thoughts and emotions.

This will be done by accepting and coming to terms with all that is lost, eliminating worry and having a positive plan for the future, but most of all enjoying now. So that by the end of this book you will be happier, have more friends, be better company, have the potential to earn much more money and be healthier and fitter.

You cannot do this in one day. You will need to read and re-read. Even better, listen to motivational tapes in your car or on your personal stereo. So that by repetition the new thought processes will be established and a gradual but very pronounced change will take place within you.

5. Most 'excess luggage' is manifested as stress

Stress is the word in common usage to describe the ill-effects of a very potent package of chemicals released within the body which is essential to survival. However, stress will cause conflict, interpersonal and intrapersonal. Stress will shorten your life. Stress causes illness, up to 75% of all illnesses. Stress causes mental breakdown. Sometimes it causes permanent mental breakdown.

You can control your emotions. You can control stress.

The stress reaction is essential to survival. It is brought about by a surge of a complex cocktail of chemicals within the body, to prepare it for defence through fight or flight. It occurs with stunning immediacy in response to shock or fright. Before you can turn to identify the source of a loud bang behind you, your heart is racing, you are breathing deeply and shaking. All in the fraction of a second.

This natural stress can be dealt with because the cause can be identified. But even at this level pre-programmed reasons will cause some to over-react. The reaction will be seen as irrational to the observer.

Herein lies the potential for stress to damage. Subconscious programming as a result of past episodes or events triggers the release of this cocktail of chemicals on an inappropriate occasion where threat is perceived but does not actually exist because the situation is matched to a similar one in the subconscious memory-bank. Sometimes, the threat has not even been consciously perceived so the reaction cannot be explained.

Many books on the subject will blame overweight, alcohol, coffee, cigarettes, food or lack of fitness, as causes of stress. While all of these affect one's ability to cope with stress or may even enhance the effects or increase the frequency of episodes, they are not the cause in themselves. The cause is within one's own subconscious, one's own over-reaction to an otherwise normal situation. Any situation that you or I find stressful will be found not stressful to most other people. In fact some people may positively enjoy the exact situation which you or I find stressful. So, stress is either a conscious judgement or a subconscious judgement of a situation. There is no stress in the situation itself. Bad news inside an envelope, for example, has already happened. You can keep the envelope for a week unopened almost knowing what is inside it and still not be affected by the news it contains. Yet as soon as you open it you become stressed or depressed. It is not the news that has made you so, it is how you are dealing with the situation. Would you open your bank statements on a Saturday?

◇

6 On the source of stress

Have you the will to change? If you know yourself honestly then you will know that you are unnecessarily stressed.

List occasions and situations when you are feeling stressed and then control them.

In periods of quiet reflection you should be able to identify the causes by slowly and methodically searching through your life, all of which is there somewhere in your memory. This will be explained in more detail later.

You can overcome stress. Never doubt that.

There are many acceptable fears and phobias in life such as fear of flying or heights or spiders. However, there are many unacceptable fears.

I believe that some fears may have a genetic origin. For example, the fact that so many people have a fear of spiders, could indicate that our ancestors were afraid of spiders, because it was only those who were afraid who survived; the others died because they were bitten by spiders. However, even this genetic fear can be overcome if you have the will to change. Through self-control, you can learn to like spiders, even to stroke them.

Perhaps the source of the most deep-seated stress reaction which is almost impossible to locate in the sub-conscious during regression, is in the womb. When a baby is in the womb it shares its mother's chemical controls. It is not itself affected by many external stimuli, except of course ingested chemicals such as drugs and alcohol. It does, however, sense touch and sound. So if a mother is subjected to beatings which would be associated with great noise the child will register the fear of the stress associated with the trauma and the noise.

Much lower down the scale but of equal significance may be traumatic circumstances such as the fear of a dentist. Where the mother's fear may be associated with the sounds and registered deep down in a way that the individual will find difficult to understand in later life. It has taken a chemical memory from the mother through sharing the mother's blood and its chemistry.

7. The damage of stress

Stress as we have seen causes the release of a whole package of chemicals which are capable of altering the function of virtually every part of the body. These obviously have beneficial effects also but when it is an unnecessary response and occurs too frequently, damage will occur to the body.

Stress lowers the body's resistance to diseases. It will lead to exhaustion both physical and mental. It affects the body's response to pain. There is a reduction in sex hormone release and the resultant loss in libido. Eating disorders will result in either over-eating through sugar requirement, or under-eating due to interference with the digestive system. There is an increase in cholesterol in the blood with all the problems that that brings. Prolonged stress will also lead to high blood pressure. It will render a person more prone to strokes, heart attacks and blood clots. And in the long term it will affect one's mental capacity in decision-making etc.

8 On depression

There are some very unpleasant deep-seated genetic or pathological depressive states from which sufferers would give anything to escape.

There is of course the great depression of grief and bereavement and other great loss. This is not to be associated with my comments below. But it still applies that in coming to terms with this enormous sense of loss, comfort is found in happy memories.

I was surprised when I read in Cleese and Skinner's books that depressed people are not sad. But having thought about it I realized how true this was – that depression in its less severe forms is a kind of self-indulgence.

Can you recall as a child having a sulk or cry and spending hours on your own in your room telling yourself how no-one loves you. Was there not a little perverse pleasure in being able to find yet another reason to add to your list of deprivations? Associated with this self-indulgence was attention seeking: 'Look at me how hurt I am . . .'; 'Look what you have done to me . . .'

If you decide to have a bad day, do you resent anyone trying to intrude into your private self-indulgent self-talk?

When you think about it, you will find that on such occasions you have switched into this frame of mind on a whim. Maybe it was because of some simple comment that you could easily have let go – as you would have done in many other cases. Is it not true that you walk away from opportunities to get out of this frame of mind.

A similar search to that discussed under stress would help you to find the pre-programmed causes for depression in many of these cases. These can be dealt with also.

◇

9. Who do you talk to most each day?

Yourself. Throughout the day, every moment you are alone, you are talking to yourself in your mind. This is called SELF-TALK. The content of this self-talk is very important. Is it negative or is it positive?

How long do you spend each day going over things that have happened wishing they were different? Or arguing with someone, in your mind, over some real or imagined problem? You can see people doing this when walking in the street or riding on a bus. You can see their facial expressions change into a scowl or sometimes into a smile. I have already mentioned the power that changing your thoughts has on mood and physical well-being. You have to work on changing and controlling your self-talk and therefore eliminating guilt and worry and developing a positive attitude.

It is said that 90% of any day's self-talk is repetition of that of the previous day. What a waste unless it is positive!

10 Why do you feel the way you do today?

Perhaps you had an unpleasant dream last night. Sometimes we get flashbacks to the dream from the previous night of which we may or may not be conscious, which may suddenly alter our mood for better or for worse. So it is important to understand our dreams – a topic I will discuss later.

Perhaps you feel the way you do today because of family problems.

Today's mood may just be due to a hangover from childhood. All human relationships depend very much on our formative years, so once again this aspect needs to be understood and investigated. This is something you can do yourself in many cases.

Or you may be anxious about what lies ahead today. People you must meet; things you must do. Why?

You must of course never ignore medical reasons for feeling 'under the weather'. There are many commonly missed medical conditions which lead to people feeling under par without their realizing it. For example: anaemia, diabetes, thyroid dysfunction, vitamin deficiencies etc. So a thorough medical check-up with a good physician is very important for everyone.

No-one can be lucky enough to have a totally uncomplicated life but the way we face the challenges of life is important. We make things much more unpleasant or very much easier just by our frame of mind.

By visualizing nice things we feel good. By visualizing unpleasant things we can feel very bad.

You are setting out on a period of self-discovery. A period of time when you will come to terms with all the negative feelings which haunt you. A period when you can accept all the wrongs that were done to you and accept all the foolish and stupid things which you have done and said in the past.

11 When you decide to change

You do not have to tell anyone anything. Just use your self-talk to talk yourself back to happiness and relaxation.

A little example: how many times when something goes wrong do you indulge in self-pity saying, why does it always happen to me? For everything that goes wrong with you in life many things go well, but even when something goes unexpectedly well do you ever stop, and with the same force of emotion, say: 'How come I am so lucky; things just seem to go right for me?' Try it.

Collect together all the things that go well and all the things that you are good at, then put them into a litany and say them to yourself many times a day over and over.

☐ I am good at running.

☐ I am good at cooking.
☐ I am very good at painting.
☐ I am a very good carpenter.
☐ I am super in bed.

Make up your own list. Do not include any criticism of anyone else, do not have any negative words in your thoughts just pure, simple, positive self-talk.

12 Write your own CV

In recent years, a business has grown in the production of CVs for people. There is now an accepted format for CVs which most people would at first feel too self-conscious or even embarrassed to use for themselves.

I recently read a batch of such CVs, some of which run to a number of pages. Each sentence, every phrase, begins with the word 'I'.

They unashamedly use phrases such as:

I am an excellent negotiator.
I am regarded as a near genius at . . .
I single-handedly led a team . . .
I was identified as being outstanding in . . .

Each project in one's working life is broken down into every component part and presented in such terms. 'I. . .', 'I. . .', 'I. . .'

This is what you need in the privacy of your own self-talk.

Write your own CV in these terms and recite it over and over again to yourself.

◇

13 On visualizing change

Before you set out on any task use your positive thoughts to set you in the right frame of mind. Then visualize the task being completed satisfactorily and it will go well. We will talk about this later. This is motivation.

On television, throughout the year, we watch athletes motivating themselves. We hear them talk of motivation. We hear of team captains giving pep talks to their team. We see tennis-players going through rituals of adjusting their shirts, hopping, bouncing the ball, to help focus their minds while they visualize the next service. We can observe and overhear the self-talk.

We heard Greg Norman talk of being totally focused on his game in the British Open in 1993. We saw glimpses of the great British rugby team being guided through their game in the dressing-room before the game, visualizing every move. We see the concentration of our great athletes living their races before they leave the blocks.

The examples are endless. Top people motivate themselves by positive self-talk and visualizing success.

☞ *It is remarkable that while so many people know how to get the best from themselves so few do it.*
Those who do, succeed.

This will be explained as the book progresses particularly in 95 and 96.

> You are a unique being there is not another in the world the same as you; therefore you have talents that no-one else has in quite the same way.
> You have a duty to yourself if not to society to identify these talents and then develop them to your greatest advantage.

14 On quality

I recently read a book entitled *Zen and the Art of Motorcycle Maintenance* by Robert Pirsig. Mr Pirsig agonized through a long period of his life over a definition of quality.

It provoked in me thoughts about the talk that we hear so much about these days regarding our quality of life both at home and at work. I will try to express my thoughts in the form of a little story.

There was a very successful well-educated businessman who was a well-known patron of the arts. Everything in his life was done with thought and taste. In his business he produced sought-after goods and he treated his staff as he did his family which to him was his most precious possession.

In his home he had a small museum to show his collection of art at its best, but only to his friends. He recently acquired a Ming vase and it was placed in pride of place in a newly-built wing of his museum. The museum although small was tastefully lavish yet did not compete with the artefacts which it housed. The staff were sophisticated and knowledgeable. This quality piece of art was indeed in the right place.

The businessman held a small party for his friends when he finally put his vase on show in the new wing. As his curator gave a talk on the dynasty in which the vase was made, one of the guests picked up the vase and after some time proclaimed it was a clever copy.

Suddenly, this worthless piece of clay mocked the gathering, mocked its owners and the building in which it stood. It mocked the quality which it was supposed to signify.

So wherein quality?

This piece was made for the wrong reasons. It was made for gain alone. It was fraudulent. Perhaps it was made just for pretence and show.

If something is done for these reasons alone it has no real quality.

Is quality, therefore, in the materials from which the vase was made? There can be quality in the materials if they are made for reasons of trying to achieve perfection; in the pursuit of excellence. Otherwise they are not worthy. The artist will seek perfection in his materials and in his technique.

A piece of art is an expression of emotion by the artist and therefore the quality of that piece is in the spirit of the artist and in the spirit of those who made the materials.

But the measure of the quality is a judgement by others. Those who empathize with the emotions expressed will see it as good quality, others will disagree.

Should we be concerned about such judgements?

The product we are discussing in this book is you. If you honestly understand the emotions you are expressing and they are being expressed totally for unselfish reasons then, without doubt, there is quality in your existence.

15 So where do you start?

We said earlier that many people carry what we can call 'excess baggage' around in their heads. It is not possible to think clearly with so much guilt, anger, worry, rows etc going on. So your mind needs a little tidying up first of all, or a good spring-cleaning.

When you are spring-cleaning, before you do the final touches like cleaning the windows and polishing the brasses, you first remove all the heavy dirt.

Perhaps a better analogy would be re-doing a derelict house where there is a lot of dirt and rubbish to be cleaned out before you can see where the real challenges are required. Are there structural repairs to be carried out before renovating, lest the whole house will fall down after all the hard work? So, how do you start?

16 The first step in relaxing

I have always found that after a busy day or after long meetings which require concentration, particularly if those meetings are in the evening, that it is hard to sleep with so much going on in my head.

I have found it very useful to sit down after a meeting, or when I come home, to write everything down that is on my mind that needs to be followed up.

I keep a pen and some paper beside me at night so when I awaken with some thoughts, or remembering something I must do, rather than lie awake saying I must not forget, I write it down. This has a very relaxing effect and can be developed into a technique for all of your day and will be addressed later.

So now write it all down.

What is worrying you? How do you feel?

Having cleared some of the excess baggage – the heavy dirt – it may come back. As you re-develop your house, walls are knocked down, ceilings are taken down, and in the process the floor it is soon covered again. It goes without saying, therefore, that the floor must be cleared constantly. This is a necessary but refreshing task.

In other words, as you delve deeper into your mind new, perhaps unpleasant, discoveries will undoubtedly appear. Unless you address and discard them they will impede your progress.

17 Meditation and family life

Now take a few minutes to relax, not to sleep but to meditate. See yourself as a child. It is not important when – just focus on a day sometime, somewhere.

See yourself with or without your parents.
Relive that day slowly, calmly.
Study yourself.
How do you feel? – Are you happy? – Who is there? – What are you doing? – Perhaps you are alone. Why? Where are you? – Are you sad? – Where is everybody?

Spend some time with these thoughts..
Do this every time you have the opportunity.
Pick another time and study your past life.

As we have seen, this is like knocking down the ceilings onto your clean floor; some unpleasant thoughts will appear – these must be confronted and dealt with.

Everybody talks about their childhood. The good bits and the bad. I did every time I met with my brothers and sisters, and I am sure my children do already when my wife and I are not there.

What you have to realize is that your parents did as they knew best. Even if they beat you or abused you they were weak and maybe useless human beings but they had never learned better.

I already feel that I have not been the best parent or even the best husband, but I have done as I thought best at any time.

I feel this way not because I have reacted in anger to any of my family, but perhaps because I should have spent more time at home to help with schoolwork or just to play games.

My children will judge and I hope forgive.

None of us will ever get it right. So, keeping that in mind, forget blaming your parents and everyone else in your childhood.

Say many times to yourself: I understand – I am weak myself – they should have known better – I hope I get it right.

Understand that your parents felt just as you have done many times, stressed – worried – guilty.

In our childhood we see adults as being totally in control. As we grow up we never feel much different than when we were children.

Where is this confidence that comes with age? It does not come easily and for many people not at all.

So sit and relax totally, regress through your life. Knock down the ceilings and clear the floor. *You clear the floor by accepting and forgiving everything.*

The roots of your guilt, your anxieties and phobias lie in the debris – clear it out. Do not waste another minute fighting over it, fretting over it; the new stuff will look much better.

As you lie in this meditative state, recite your own litany of all you are good at many times to yourself so that, gradually, it begins to replace in your subconscious some of the debris you are discarding.

We have already seen that, through constant repetition, we can re-programme ourselves so that now, as space becomes available in your subconscious mind, you can start moving in the new building materials.

Repeat over and over to yourself (your own check-list):-

- ☐ I am a good carpenter
- ☐ I am a good cook
- ☐ I am a good lawyer
- ☐ I am a good driver
- ☐ I am a good typist

Now, in this short time:

a) You have accepted that you can change.
b) You have seen the power of the mind over the body.
c) The wastefulness of worry, guilt etc.
d) How you can change mood by visualization.
e) The need for a positive frame of mind.
f) How top athletes control their bodies.
g) How to eliminate or deal with worry.
h) How to come to terms with your childhood.

i) Most important – how to start to lay the foundations for positive thought.

Everything you do in life deserves to be prepared for so that the best possible outcome can be achieved.

> At this point you might find it very helpful to re-read the last few pages again because there is a lot to absorb.

You could now add some of your desires into your litany:

'I am very slim.'
'I am fit.'
'I have a sense of humour' etc.

Visualize this different you. Do not try to change. For example, do not try to give up smoking, let it be your intention for the moment. When your mind is right you will stop.

DO NOT TRY – LET IT HAPPEN – RELAX

Have you ever picked up the phone to call a friend and found you could not remember the number, try as you might it will not come back? You try to force it out. It is on the tip of your tongue but it will not come.

Someone says leave it a moment, it will come when you start to think of something else.

It usually does, doesn't it? The information is stored but the harder you try the less well the brain works. You must relax, take in all the necessary information and it will become assimilated in your mind and the solutions will suddenly come as soon as you are ready.

18 On making decisions

People talk about making a decision. 'I will sit down this afternoon and decide.' Or 'The Committee will meet next week to decide.' This is nonsense, you cannot force a decision; it is either a consensus view or a 'snap decision'. The way proper decisions are 'made' is to collect all the necessary information, study it well and relax and then the decision will happen.

If you think about the best things you have done in your life you may find that you woke up one morning and the answer was there, as if it was by chance.

People say they did it on a whim, or they had a gut feeling for a certain project, or it was love at first sight, or they saw it and just had to have it. This is because the mind was ready and the message was there. Were you listening?

How many times is it said: 'Something deep down was telling me not to get involved but I did, I wish I had gone by my instinct.' Clear your mind – take in all the necessary information and relax and suddenly, when you least expect it, there is your solution.

[Decision-making is discussed again in section .]

Begin to relax. Start to remove some of those things which have been burdening your mind and start to come to terms with the guilt and blame that have been holding you back. Think about how you are at present and how you relate to other people.

No man is an island. No-one has a right to (or should) live in isolation while depending on the community to support him.

We all have talents and abilities and we have a duty to develop these and use them to our own advantage while contributing to the community as well.

◇

19 Understanding blame; understanding 'you PLC'

Look at yourself as Business. 'YOU PLC'. You are the complete business. You the Managing Director, you the computer, you the factory and the equipment. You are responsible for public relations and sales, you are responsible for buying, you are maintenance. Every aspect of this business – YOU PLC – is you. No-one else is to blame for what takes place. So you must look at the business and analyse its performance.

We live in hard times, you may be out of work so you say: 'Not my fault I am broke old boy. ME PLC is out of business.' You are wrong; whatever you went broke for is only one department of 'YOU PLC' gone out of production, you have to open another. 'YOU PLC' can produce many products; it is a multi-faceted company with tremendous resources. So you must have a board meeting and change directions. (You are lucky the State will give you some money to feed yourself while you do some restructuring.)

How is the Managing Director – The Mind? Is he bogged down with guilt and worry or is he giving leadership?

You have discovered while you meditated on your life that your father beat you, or your mother did not give you enough affection. So the Managing Director – The Mind – cannot run your PLC properly. Does this make sense? No, you cannot let this hatred or feeling of having been cheated preoccupy you. Forgive immediately and then move on.

Though we travel the world to find the beautiful, we must carry it with us or we find it not.

EMERSON

20 | Dealing with problems

Drop the word *problem* from your vocabulary; from today there will only be challenges. Problem denotes a reason for not proceeding but a challenge implies the excitement of looking for a solution. We hear it every day: 'Ah, but it cannot be done because....' 'Have WE got a problem!'

Have you ever secretly thought: 'Oh, great! The car won't start.' or 'Oh, great. The power has gone off so I can go home.' or 'Oh, great. My secretary is sick so I can't work.' Or, if you are at home – the power is off so you don't have to do any housework. Or, you have mislaid your wallet so you are secretly pleased not to have to go shopping. Or, when you wake up with a slightly sore throat which helps you to build an excuse to have a day off work.

Remember, however, you must be honest with yourself if you genuinely wish to change.

Do not secretly welcome a problem. Always be positive in seeking a solution to a challenge. Indeed, you will almost certainly grow to enjoy the challenge.

21 | How do you maintain your body (your PLC)?

We are back to 'YOU PLC' and the good news is that the Managing Director is getting a grip. How is the equipment – you? Are you fit, are you over-weight, do you smoke or drink too much? The business cannot work too well with badly-maintained equipment. Now is the time for honesty: you are, after all, reporting to the board.

I was once 17 stone (240 pounds) and a friend said one day: 'Joe that's awful, look at the button bursting on your shirt'. I was not upset, I just took it on board and thought about it. When I looked in the mirror I began to see the real shape, not the one I had become used to. One morning I got up, looked in the mirror and said: 'That's it' and went on a diet. Over the next few months I lost four stone (56 pounds). I took up running and after a short time I ran a marathon. I never planned either, I just saw what I had become and I did not like it. So I thought about it and one day I started to change. In that same period I stopped enjoying cigarettes and stopped wanting to smoke. I never planned that.

◇

22 How are you packaged?

So a new plan is emerging for the plant and equipment. How is the product you are producing? Maybe not selling at all. You are out of a job. You need a new product.

If the product is not selling very well what is the reason? Is your skill needed? If not, then perhaps you need to plan for the future. Perhaps the product – you – is not well packaged, does not make others feel good. Are you giving the wrong signals? Do you pose a threat to others? (This is discussed further under Dress [31], Body Language [33] and

Making meetings worthwhile 92.)

So how is 'YOU PLC' in the Customer Service Department? You must remember that the customer is always right. The customer has a similar number of hang-ups to yours, not the same ones necessarily but in equal or greater amounts and if they have not come to terms with their life then you will be burdened with this. So how you react to these people and situations decides how easy your passage through life will be.

'Do unto others as you would that they do unto you' is as important a saying 2,000 years on. Later in the book we will look at human relationships.

23 | Feeding body and mind

We also said that 'YOU PLC' had a Buying Department for which you are entirely responsible. You are in control. You are preparing the information, all the research is done by you before a decision is made. This of course includes education. If you feel you are lacking in education in any field this can lead to feeling inferior – not being prepared. There are adult education courses to help you here. Every bit of input is very valuable.

We need to look at what you are feeding the body with as well as your mind. One cannot be dissociated from the other. Indeed, food can have a profound affect on the *state of mind.*

Many people have mapped their lives, including all the food intake, drink, weather, time of year, time of the month and time of day etc, to see what affected them and how it affected them. All of these items do have very noticeable effects. A clear example is jet-lag where the circadian rhythms are severely disrupted resulting in very pronounced and unpleasant symptoms.

Our bodies are conditioned by our routines; to the extent that we do not really need an alarm clock in the morning, to the time of eating, going to the toilet, going to bed.

◇

24 Preparing for everything in life

We are better at certain things, at certain times of the day. Try keeping a diary and learn your body rhythms. Use these to your advantage. Why go to a meeting when you are not at your best – you would not go and get drunk prior to a very important meeting so why would you eat something that is not good for you or go at the wrong time of day? And why would you go without improving your mind? You must first take in all the necessary information, then get yourself in the right frame of mind. Say to yourself:

- ☐ I am good at interviews
- ☐ I understand my body
- ☐ I understand the interviewers

☐ I am the right person for the job
☐ And I am good in bed

All this time continue to clear out the debris of your mind to make room for positive input. You must start to lay plans for 'YOU PLC'. The Forward Planning Department is the most important. Start to build a picture of where you want to be and *who do you want to be*.

Sometimes in meditation or in your dreams, the picture is very clear. You need to build a similarly clear picture in your mind, of what you want. When that picture is clear – when you visualize in absolute clarity what you want, then it will happen. Getting that picture right takes a lot of time in the early stages. A time with no apparent productivity. You cannot have productivity without planning and the planning must be as near perfect as you can make it.

If you are building a house, the foundations and all the materials must be precise and top quality, otherwise it would not last any time. Now that you are rebuilding yourself you have got to get it right. This begins at the planning stage, then you continue to use only the best materials and the best workmanship to build a lasting desirable product. A new you.

'Unless a man be born again'. Another quotation from a great philosopher, Christ. I am not a deeply religious man but I do believe in some form of spiritual Being, about which I will talk later. We cannot ignore the wisdom of those great men whose words are still significant even 2000 years later.

What we have been talking about up to now is rebirth, the new product from 'YOU PLC'.

25 Responsibility to a new-born baby

When a baby is conceived it does not have hang-ups or phobias, it has no guilt, it has no knowledge. It is just like buying a new computer where the electronics are in place but there is no information. For the computer we carefully choose the best programme, the one that best suits the machine and the one that will do the job required.

With regard to a baby, how often is the job done with so much thought? From the moment a baby opens its eyes for the first time it is receiving input, the programming begins.

This first input becomes very important in later life because at this stage a baby needs contact and needs to communicate. It does not know any words so its initial communication is by tone, sound and facial expressions. We all recognize a happy voice from a sad or angry voice, happy music from sad music; we also know a happy face from a sad face and indeed, all the variations in between. There are very many muscles making up the face, head and neck which will act in hundreds of combinations and will easily reveal our true feelings. A baby will quickly become well-versed in interpreting the finest variations in facial expression. This information will be carried and used for the rest of its life.

Other important influences in the child's programming are affection, sympathy, its environment and many others. So the early formative years which are so important are controlled by the parents and therefore their state of mind is very important.

26 On childhood

If a child has not had a good childhood then the preparation for life has not been done properly and the person is not ready to be an adult. He or she will almost certainly go through life with hang-ups, the feelings of deprivation and inferiority, guilt, anxiety and all the problems we have been discussing. Of course one may be lucky enough to receive sufficient love later in life to compensate for earlier deprivation. So many people can live reasonably normal lives because of the love and support of a good marriage. Herein may lie the cause of so many marriage breakdowns – when two people are seeking the same support and are not able to give enough.

One must be allowed to be a child again and to be built up again with the love and attention that was missing the first time.

We find relaxation by being 'childish' at times. When groups of men or women get together socially the best fun is quite often described as 'silly'. In fact the better we know people the more we are prepared to 'let our hair down' in their company, and some of the best evenings at dinner parties fall into this category. This is very therapeutic.

So, as you start to rebuild the new you it is essential to have love and support in a happy environment, and you can see that it is important to regress in your relaxation back to a very early stage in your life if you are to find all the causes of your present state of mind.

We are not discussing blame we are just trying to discover the causes of our problems and come to terms with all that is unpleasant and clear it out. The more you clear out the better because a relaxed mind is essential and the relaxed mind will be amazingly productive.

◇

27 On re-birth

This re-birth you are undergoing obviously has a purpose. You have a desire to change your life and yourself. You know what that 'new' you will be. Spend some time visualizing the new you. You need to build a crystal-clear picture of what you want and gather all the information you require. Gradually, the urge to proceed with what you want will be so great that you will have no option but to go with it. Remember, do not try to change except in acquiring the necessary information.

When we talked about the baby observing facial expressions it was the repetition that ingrained the information in its mind, and throughout life repetition is the system by which we learn and store information. It is through repetition that the new information will be logged in your mind. Continuous visualization of the new you is essential as is the continuous recitation of the litany of what you are good at – your CV. Building positive self-talk is also an essential part of your re-birth.

28 On self-consciousness

How do you feel when you walk up into a group of people? For example, you are going to a party or to a dinner or you are going for an interview. Your programming as a baby and as a child has conditioned you to make certain snap decisions about everyone you meet.

The children in the poem, *The Village Schoolmaster*, 'learned to anticipate the day's disasters from his morning face'.

We have talked about the complexity of the musculature of the head and neck and how as a child you learned how to interpret facial expressions. Being aware of how you can betray your thoughts by facial expression you have also learned to mask these signs.

You can be poker-faced so that you leave everyone guessing what is going on in your head. You can give an almost imperceptible signal across a crowded room to a partner or someone you know well. You will have learned to smile when you meet people to put them at ease.

29 | On first impressions

But before you mask your signals when you meet someone there is a split second when the real you is exposed. So when you meet people and form a snap decision of what they are really like it is quite often accurate. First impressions are known to be a very good guide, particularly to someone good at reading facial expression and body language because you get a glimpse – a snapshot – of their tensions and anxieties. These emotions are betrayed by just the minutest movement of a muscle.

30 | On role-play

Also as a child you learned to imitate certain role-plays in each encounter. You learned to act as a child, as an adult or as an equal; and of course you learned to role-play in different ways with men and women. So that in that first few seconds of an encounter with another person you will have set the pecking order for that relationship, will you be the child to their adult or vice-versa, or as an equal. Will you treat the other person as a mother/father figure, sister/brother figure, or flirt with them?

You must remember also that these people all have their own hang-ups, their own feelings of inadequacy and are making their judgement of you and what role they will play. So sometimes people are immediately incompatible.

While it is important to discover and sort out what causes you to give the wrong signals to others it is also important to learn to mask your real feelings and of course to set a good state of mind before every encounter. It is important that when you first meet people that they do not feel threatened by you, unless of course that is your intention.

The first thing to do, therefore, is to set a frame of mind so that you will be happy and positive. Use positive self-talk – 'I am happy; I feel good; I am good company' etc. Say it over and over to yourself. Before entering a room or a meeting make your entry positively in the desired frame of mind.

31 On dress

Another very important thing is dress. Women are better at knowing what to wear and dress to suit the occasion without feeling over- or under-dressed. For men it is similarly important in social settings but more so in business or meetings and interviews. One does not go to the bank to borrow money looking too expensively turned out with gold showing in watches, rings etc. The bank manager earns a certain amount of money and may be made to feel inferior if your clothes are overpowering. Secondly, expensive clothes and jewelry are signs that you may not be cautious with the bank's money and bank managers are usually cautious people. Thirdly, you need to dress to look professional and businesslike.

If you are going to see a customer you will not want him to think that you might be making too much money out of him. There is a delicate balance here because you need to imply that you are successful at your job but also fair in your dealings. Your clothes and your car give these signs. If, however, you wish to dominate in an encounter you must dress accordingly with more expensive clothes but not flashy and certainly no jewelry. Before you go to any of these meetings you must also 'Dress your mind' – use positive self-talk suitable to the occasion. 'I am good at my job; I am successful; these people need me.' Sit and visualize the meeting and have a clear picture of what you want as a result.

32 On understanding the problems of others

The next thing to do in an encounter is to help the other person. If you go to the bank, for example, the manager has a job to do; be aware of his side of the situation. He must protect the bank's interests and he also must protect himself. If he makes ill-prepared applications for lending to his head office it affects his promotion. If he makes too many bad loans he loses his job. You must be prepared for all meetings, have all the necessary information and present it confidently in a relaxed way in order to reduce anxiety in the other party.

Similarly, if you are stopped by policeman he has a job to do and if you help him in that then life could be a lot easier for you.

We all know that one comment can change the whole tone of a conversation. You may say to your partner: 'I didn't much like that dinner', to which there are two types of reply: 'I'm sorry, I won't cook that again', or 'If you don't like it do it yourself in future', and that comment can have two different types of reply: 'I'm sorry I didn't mean to offend you.' [problem gone], or 'Don't talk to me like that.' [You can work out the rest of the evening from there yourself.] Apply these analogies to all your encounters.

So we can control how encounters will go by defusing tension or adding to it. 'Do unto others as you wish they would to you.'

In doing this you can control your own mood. Having had a row with someone how do you feel? You may say with satisfaction, 'I told him what I thought of him', but what is the point when you feel bad all day yourself afterwards and your mind is occupied with this row going on over and over again. The opposite is also true. If you help people and are nice to them it gives a good feeling and this good feeling always seems to be far greater than the cost to you or the effort involved.

It is far nicer to give than to receive, isn't it? Is not the fun of watching someone open and enjoy a gift far greater than being watched opening your gift? It would seem, therefore, that to have happiness you just have to give and help others. Acknowledge their weaknesses and understand their inner feelings.

33 On body language

Another thing to learn to understand and control is body language. As noted earlier, you give clear signals to others by the way you walk and use your hands and legs, or the way you hold your head.

If you see someone walking down the street with his shoulders bent forward and his head down you know he is unhappy. Similarly with someone walking with back straight and head up you know he is confident. But there are more subtle signs. Is the person to whom you are talking, for example, showing signs of stress? If so, he may scratch the back of his head. Is he being defensive with his arms blocking you out? This is done in varying degrees from an arm across the body to the arms folded.

The person may show signs of needing reassurance or that they are out of their depth by the degree to which they stroke themselves – usually involving hand contact with the face or hair. When joining others in company you are giving as many signals as you receive. You have set the pecking order. So it is obviously important to give the correct signals and then to live up to those signals. Be aware that you can talk to another person's subconscious, by controlling the information from your face and body language to make him feel more comfortable. The good actors are those who have learned to master the facial muscles to convey the mood they wish to project.

Friends talking will mimic the body language of each other so that greater harmony exists between them. You can observe close friends who have copied each others gestures, as of course do married couples and their children.

34 On the new you

So where does all this get the new you? It is important that the new you is so clearly ingrained in your subconscious that it is projected in every way from your tone of voice, your gestures, facial expressions and what you say. This may sound like a fraud, it would be if you were an actor in all of your life masking the real you; but if you are creating a new you then what you are projecting will be the signs of that person you want to be. This is the public relations and the sales department of 'YOU PLC'.

> Here is an interesting point to contemplate: Why do you like some people and dislike others? You dislike those who threaten you. Why are they a threat? Obviously they are a threat if they are going to hurt you or take your money; but it maybe that they are a threat because they trigger some subconscious conditioned reaction by their body language. Or they give signs of contesting your assumed dominance in a particular situation, this being done by subconscious signals. These situations are well worth exploring in your meditation. This is not to say that you should ignore or suppress these useful signals but you must be aware of what is going on.

35 On inferiority

Why do you feel inferior? Perhaps you do not feel inferior but strive to establish superiority throughout all your activities. This may stem from inferiority. Inferiority stems from childhood deprivation of affection and approval. There is nothing wrong with striving to succeed, but it is important to come to terms with the reasons why. It may take away some of the unnecessary and unproductive even counter-productive striving to compete in every situation. When you close your eyes to reflect on your childhood spend some time on this point. Having acknowledged the cause, it will take much of the stress out of your activities and leave all your efforts to be used in a worthwhile way.

36 On being civilized

There are many outside stimuli which control us in a subconscious way in our daily life. We are controlled by music, colour and smell in many places that we go to, from the supermarkets to airports. We must never forget that civilization is the suppression and control of instinctive behaviour to enable social co-existence to take place. It does not take away the basic animal instinct within us. This can be observed by the way we are affected by weather and time of the year, and also how we react in crowds, to how we react when we board a bus, or go into a doctor's waiting room: which seat we choose is not random but depends on many factors – for example, who was sitting in a particular seat, male or female, before us.

It is observed that on some days everyone will arrive early for their appointment and on other days they will be late, and yet other days many people will cancel their appointments. Similarly, on certain days many will be depressed and on others they will be anxious or argumentative.

It is good to be aware of these stimuli which affect you and use the information to your advantage. For example, there used to be a time at airports when there was the constant noise of information over loudspeakers, which had a very tiring effect on the staff and affected the way they dealt with customers, who in turn were increasingly irritated by the loudspeaker noise. Now it is gone. Instead, we must watch the screens for information. So the staff are healthier because of the reduced stress and the public are easier to control.

In public places, using again the example of an airport where people are not required to wait, there are no seats, and the colour and the decor is not conducive to lingering so people move on. However, the shops' area is much more comfortable, carpeted, and also smells nice with perhaps some soothing background music playing so that you will linger a while and spend your money. The dedicated waiting areas are similarly laid out and inviting so that the public is easier to manage. As you walk to the plane you are guided easily by coloured carpets.

Similarly in your own life, you will find outside stresses which must be eliminated. For example, reduce noise in the workplace and substitute with soothing music. I have found that instead of pop music which can be too noisy for relaxed working, young people will choose the earlier classical composers like Correlli or Bach or Vivaldi rather than those from later periods. This is because of the simplicity of the music and its purity. However, we will all find some music that is more soothing than the rest. But during periods of intense concentration even this music can be an intrusion.

We can all do many jobs in our mind at once. For example, when attending a lecture, we can listen and write, but what we are writing is what we heard a few moments ago, so we must listen, store and produce all at the same time. We can also count while we are doing other things.

It is possible to drive a car, watch the road, listen to the radio and hold a conversation at the same time, but when an emergency occurs or when you are lost and cannot find the way the conversation stops, the radio goes off as the stress of concentration sets in.

So establish a comfortable work-place and

of course a comfortable home. It is hard to relax in an untidy environment. It is important to be mindful of comfort for all the senses.

37 More on the new you

You can see the need to get your surroundings organized, the people and the environment in readiness for the new you. The new you will be slim and fit and healthy and good at your job. The picture is growing of a popular friend who is relaxed and fun, and most of all successful and looks good.

The new you also needs people, the right people; real friends. You need people to support you and encourage you and to love you. All of which qualities must be reciprocated unquestioningly.

There are many others who will not fall into this category but because they cannot support you they are not your enemy, they have just too many problems of their own. Understanding this will make life easier for you and perhaps a little easier for them.

There are those who are continually seeking sympathy and attention. They will tell you of their problems each time you see them. These people are completely opposite to the new you. They enjoy their illnesses, their depression is self-indulgent. No matter how often these people talk about their problems it does not help them to come to terms with them.

I saw recently a very striking demonstration of self-limitation in a demonstration on hypnosis. A man was hypnotized and told that he would not be able to hear anything until he was told otherwise. While he was in this state he could not hear anything yet he could hear the hypnotist. He was not deaf but he could not hear.

It is possible also to be similarly unable to see, as in hysterical blindness. Another example would be in writer's cramp.

These are examples of the power of the mind working against itself.

◇

38 Psychogenic illness

A large proportion of illnesses are in the mind, or are physical manifestations of subconscious programming. They are what are known as psychogenic illnesses, eating disorders, allergies, headaches, face-aches, abdominal problems, back trouble, impotence, incontinence and many, many others.

This is not to say that the problems are not real – they are – but the cause is in the mind. Your mind has the power to paralyse you – to stop you eating, riddle you with pain, and cause panic attacks; yet so little is done to address this 'condition'.

39 On pain

What is pain? It is the body's defence mechanism and early warning system. That is it. It should be just be between you and your doctor. But what do people talk about almost as much as the weather – their pain.

We all crave sympathy: it is a sign that we are cared for. And so, all too often, the mind produces pain and illness so that sympathy will be gained. Perhaps it was only in illness that love and sympathy and tenderness were granted in childhood. Illness is also a good excuse to avoid unpleasant activities.

If you are playing a game of football it is possible to sustain a fractured leg and not feel the pain, whereas if you were walking down the street and someone gave you a slight kick on the shin you might well end up in agony. Now there are many reasons why you react in different ways to the two incidents, but the fact is that you do. So, clearly, it is possible to control the perception of pain.

If you are having an injection it is only one prick of a very sharp needle, it does not really hurt. But most people tense up so much and focus on that tiny point on their body that it hurts very much or appears to. However, if they were to dissociate themselves from what was going on then it is possible not to feel anything.

There are many examples of this. People walking on hot coals or lying on a bed of nails.

There are perhaps many factors at play here, but it is by controlling the mind that they are able to undertake these challenges.

An athlete running a race pushes himself through pain by his desire to win or break a record but you have seen what happens at the end of the race: the winner smiles and runs a lap of honour almost as if he had not exerted himself while on the other hand, all the losers are lying on the ground gasping for breath and in pain. As they race to the line you can see the growing smile on the face of he who senses victory, while the one who knows he is defeated shows his pain.

Your pain is a personal thing; people do not really want to know about it. The question is are you going to let pain interfere with the rest of your life, or are you going to put it in its place and focus your mind on productive positive things. Repeat to yourself as often as you need to: I am fit – I am well – I am active, and other parts of your private CV.

40 | On the need for being fit

Meanwhile, back at 'YOU PLC' things are now going well. The new foundations are laid and most of the clearing up has taken place but you must keep tidying up the rubbish all the time.

We have looked at the Customer Service Department and see what the customer wants.

We have looked at the salesman and given him is instructions. The new product is well under way in design and being visualized. It is time to start working on the equipment.

Good equipment is imperative for sustained productivity, for efficient products and for morale.

Are you fit? (It is always best to have medical advice if you are very unfit and plan to take a lot of exercise suddenly.) There is no one way to go about getting fit. There is just the simple fact that you must do it. The first thing to do is to build fitness into your self-motivation, your litany of good points and your visualizations.

Visualize yourself as slim, fit, winning a race, for example. Most of the larger life forms we can think about are, in their purest or best representation, sleek, fast fit or very cunning. It is in the nature of early man to be fit. Man the hunter. Man the provider. Man at play – always fit and fast.

Today's man is none of these. We are depriving ourselves of a very important input for good living. Hunting man lived on bursts of adrenaline and endorphins (the body's own painkillers). He thrived on the need to provide – to hunt. He excelled in locating and stalking his prey. He excited in the physical activity of the chase and he thrilled in the satisfaction of the success. This is what life is about, the joys of being at one with nature, of living instinctively for the good of one's community and family.

By living instinctively I mean living by the forces within. Unfortunately, these good forces have become suppressed in most of us and the purpose of this book is to help you to rediscover the real you, the purpose of living.

◇

41 On being human

If you were to quickly (right now) write down the main advantages that you have being human over all the other animals – what would you write?

- ☐ I can communicate, read, write, talk
- ☐ I can build a nice house
- ☐ I can have a job and earn money
- ☐ I can sit and enjoy nature
- ☐ I can get all the things I like
- ☐ I can travel around the world

And so on.

Now look back at your list and see if any of the points you have written are important. Are they only important because you are human? Would your cat consider any of your points important or indeed necessarily useful in his existence?

Being human puts requirements and obligations on us that no other animal appears to have. Man is a social animal who has always lived in a society. Intelligence has made him strive for civilization in that society. Because it is through intelligence that we have reason and choice. We have the opportunity to come to terms with the basic instincts many of which must be suppressed to enable us to live in society.

42 On being intelligent

Philosophers have struggled to define intelligence. It is defined most commonly as the ability to adapt to a changing environment. From our point of view in this book, intelligence can be taken to mean being able to control our emotions, to think and be able to control our thoughts. This is the profound message. The fundamental thing to accept is that you can control your thoughts.

If thoughts are challenging emotions, is this eventually going to cause stress? It would appear better, therefore, to understand the emotions they cause and to try to remove if possible those damaging emotions.

43 What are emotions?

Emotions are how we feel as a result of the chemistry of a memory flooding through the body. They are the cornerstones of our personality. The basic memory of the most profound experience of our existence, and some are an expression of the basic instincts of our animal nature.

Firstly, let us consider those which evolve from experience. In our first days, weeks and years of life we have basic requirements: for affection, food and comfort which may be said to fulfil the requirements for love. If we are satisfied in these requirements then we are happy. If we are deprived then we become ill. But the deprivation can leave a lasting 'mental scar' in our memory.

As we go through our formative years an abnormal response to a natural desire or requirement will be logged in our memories, and similar circumstances will for ever more evoke those memories as inexplicable feelings or moods.

How often have you said or heard others say: 'I know that face – I cannot remember from where but it rings a bell.' or 'It means trouble', 'I wish I could remember'. Or when asked to describe someone, you immediately know the person, you have an aura but cannot describe the person to others. When you try you cannot even visualize the person.

Memories are chemical taggings into the brain. Their recall causes emotions.

As we saw earlier, when we are born we have certain basic needs and the way those needs are addressed lays down our emotional response for the rest of our lives. Unless, of course, we can re-visit the period of tagging of our memory of these emotions and correct or come to terms with the error.

I am not too pleased with the popular definition of intelligence which says that it is largely to do with our ability to adapt to a changing environment. So I am the highest form of animal because I can struggle to fight against an Ice Age or a flood or a drought – I don't mind the pain and the sacrifice, I am lucky to be human. I don't think so.

If being able to think is the measure, I am not too pleased to be human either. If I think about tomorrow and worry, or I think about yesterday and feel guilty and embarrassed. If I face tomorrow with anxiety what is the value of being intelligent – better to be an animal and live on instinct alone. This will get you food and a nest, satisfy your sexual drive, and perhaps a group to live in if you need it. Maybe you will get to be leader if you are good enough. Maybe you could be a worker bee and know no better and have a fulfilling life. This is not what being the highest form of life is about.

Animals have emotions. They can be happy, sad, experience fear etc. We humans can add worry, embarrassment and feelings of inadequacy and inferiority.

* * *

Unless we take control, our emotions control our thinking.

Wayne Dyer explains:

> We can control our thoughts.
> Our thoughts provoke memories.
> Memories provoke emotions.
> Therefore we can control our emotions.

I would take this one step farther. Our emotions are how we feel due to chemical changes brought on by memories. Therefore we can control our chemistry.

If we can control our chemistry we can control our physical well-being. We can control our mental well-being.

* * *

A little example:

Imagine with your eyes closed. You are on holiday. It is raining and dark. You are in your hotel room on the fourth floor. Go to the balcony and look over. Down below is a bed of nails. Suddenly, the rail breaks. You fall over.

Did you feel a jolt of pain just thinking about it? Did you feel the sinking feeling of falling? You felt the emotion. You felt the chemistry of fright rushing through your body by the power of thought.

If you felt this way all the time, living with anxiety, can you see how it must affect your body and mind?

But now, close your eyes again. Imagine you are on the same holiday on the same balcony. It is bright and sunny. You have just come up from a most pleasant day by the pool, showered and poured yourself a cold drink. Below you everything is peaceful, save for the clinking of dinner plates and the slight hum of conversation from the poolside bar. The sun is slowly sinking beneath the sea. It is so peaceful.

How do you feel? There is now a very different chemistry rushing through your veins.

It is so easy to change your mind and change how you feel. Why don't you take permanent control!

◇

44 On acting

But you must be careful here: to change thoughts without going deeper is bound to cause conflict.

An actor may play a certain character and be the character totally for many months and yet not change himself. This will tire the actor and cause stress. Pretending to be someone else is not the answer. If the real person was on stage each night his life would be very easy.

For the actor there is a conflict because the personality he is portraying is not agreeing with his own personality. Life can be the same for you if you are acting you will find life very stressful. You can change the person you are but it must be complete.

Are you fooled by the person who is always dressed very well but lives in a hovel, or the person who drives a flashy car but has no house? No? You must be the same person through and through.

45 Free will

So you can now see that the advantage – the bonus – of intelligence is to be able to think and to reason, and since we control our thoughts we have, through our intelligence, free will. You can also change previously programmed instinctive reactions.

For example, if you are driving along the road and someone steps out in front of you, you immediately slam your foot on the brakes. You do not have to think about it, there is no self-talk; it is instinctive-survival reaction. Yet you were not born knowing how to stop a car. You learned it. You practised it. It was probably the first question you asked your driving teacher, how do I stop? Because as an animal you have an instinct for survival, you therefore have a need and a desire to learn. So the ability to stop the car is learned quickly and thoroughly.

This example also demonstrates the fact that if you programme new habits and altered emotions properly they will be there silently working for your own good, controlling the new you, just as the bad emotions controlled you in the past.

By using your free will and reason you can, through your thoughts, reap the benefits of your intelligence which must simply be happiness, living and enjoying a fulfilled life. A life free of guilt and worry, of embarrassment and anxiety.

46 Mental cocoon, mental barriers and the 'comfort zone'

There are not many people who will say that they are enjoying life to the full. The most advanced animal on earth is not using its unique intelligence to make itself happy. Why not? Modern humans are generally lazy. Not lazy by nature but they live in a mental cocoon – that zone which has been called the 'comfort zone'. An area beyond which it requires effort to go, for some people this is a very small zone. Such people have a very low tolerance to most things and will not undertake anything which causes them discomfort. To think of going beyond the comfort zone causes stress. Because they do not try, the boundaries shrink around them. Eventually, stress is all around them. In section 5 I said that stress is a judgement. There is no stress at the boundaries of the comfort zone. A soon as you take action the stress is gone. Stress is in the failure to take action.

Another good example will be discussed under 'Running'.

On the other end of the scale there are those who enjoy pushing themselves to the limits and beyond. The obvious example is in athletics. Those who succeed find that the barriers are mainly mental. Athletes must have their bodies in good condition before they really start to push themselves but it is only by pushing, by self-motivation that they can achieve this level of fitness.

If you try in this area you will find that if one day you go an extra few miles or a second faster that the psychological barrier immediately begins to move. The next time you run the longer distance is the norm or the time is the norm. It is not that you have suddenly become fitter you have just adjusted your comfort zone, extended the walls of your cocoon.

This same principle applies to all aspects of life. If you want to diet it is something which will cause some discomfort. But by the power of thought, by motivation you can enjoy expanding the mental cocoon and actually feel very fulfilled by every small success.

Having taken stock of all those aspects of yourself that you would like to change the same principle applies to each one. It would not be wise, however, to try to change everything at once. As has been said several times already, you must not *try* to change because this is forcing the issue. The change will come from within.

47 Think positive, not negative

By the power of your thoughts you have to change the way you think. Remove all negativity from all thoughts. It is negativity which has set the boundaries of your mental cocoon. This requires a process of becoming much more aware of yourself, of your habits and of your self-imposed limits.

Having corrected your thinking to being positive the changes will begin to happen. Suddenly, one day, you will feel like running that extra mile or two. It will seldom be planned. This applies to mental activity, as we talked about before in relation to remembering telephone numbers. We hear of singers being told not to force their voice but to let it flow from deep down. We watch the more relaxed runner winning a race and see the loser straining himself. What is required is a desire to change and constantly visualizing the achievement of the goals and constantly thinking positively.

48 On competing

Many people when asked to help or to do something for us say they cannot – they are unable or don't know how. What they mean is they do not want to or that they do not wish to try to do what is asked of them because it would require them to move out of their comfort zone and because their negative thinking tells them that it is not possible. There are those who give glory to God, that there were so many under-achievers in the world because that meant there were more opportunities for them.

This sentiment does not have any place in

the mind of a healthy individual who wishes all others well. One does not have to compete with anyone else in the world – not even the winning athlete. He may run a tactical race and win in a time that is well short of his best. To produce his best he simply has to compete with himself but that implies effort which we have agreed is wrong. He 'competes' with himself by trying to improve on his previous best time. This must be done by self-congratulations, motivation, encouragement and a complete harmony of mind and body.

49 Something about our IQ

Our intelligence is our ability to adapt to change by interpreting input, designing an appropriate response and then expressing or executing the planned response.

Individuals are limited by attempts to measure intelligence, particularly by those systems which use only verbal and numerical components.

Recent thinking as expressed by Tony Buzane demonstrates how limiting and unjust this has been. Firstly, by depriving individuals of opportunity by such measurements. Secondly, if one firmly believes that he/she is of limited ability one will perform within that range. Thirdly, by the idea IQ (Intelligence Quotient) cannot be changed.

If you have the will to change and all the

qualities we strive for in this book then you can improve your intelligence. An individual could be what we regard as a good all-round person: good at sport, art, music, technical matters, languages, sciences, good with other people, well motivated, sensitive but lack a suitable vocabulary to express it. Under present IQ measurements they could be regarded as of low IQ. This shows the folly of present methods.

We need new ways to measure. If we look at the areas mentioned again it will be seen that you can:

1. Improve your self-motivation and thinking.
2. Develop fitness and ability at sport.
3. Learn music, art and languages.
4. Increase your vocabulary.
5. Improve the ability to deal with other people.
6. Increase your awareness of everything around you and within you.

If you can do all these things you can improve your IQ. You can do this because you can remove blocks in your interpretation of input. This will increase intuition.

By increased awareness you will receive greater and more accurate input.

By increased knowledge you will be better able to express your solutions to the challenges of your environment. These issues are considered in more detail later.

On becoming adult

So why do people not change? Were they always the way they are now? No they were not. Every baby is born the same. Born to be happy and with the potential to do many things. They love fun and adventure and learning. They love activity and they have almost boundless energy. They dream most of the day and they are for that day what they dream to be. Their cardboard box is a jet one day and a submarine or a palace in the woods the next.

A child will take any piece of equipment and say 'I can do it'. They see the world as it is and say 'I can do anything and be happy'. Then something goes wrong. Adults interfere and put limits on the child. Some very necessary for survival but others come out of the parents' self-imposed limits.

The boundaries of their cocoon begin to be laid down. Negativity sets in. We should look at the child as the teacher and learn to dream to have no self-imposed boundaries. We should learn to say I can do anything. This is the state of mind you need to return to.

Children like to laugh a lot. Do they laugh because they are happy or are they happy because they laugh? We are told that laughter is very therapeutic. It relieves stress and in fact is a very quick way to resolve a stressful situation; simply tell a joke everyone laughs and the atmosphere changes. So a better working environment is established. Children are very energetic and fit.

Most highly-motivated people keep their body in shape as well as their minds, in fact it would seem essential for proper functioning of the mind to indulge in reasonably strenuous exercise many times a week if not each day.

This requires for most people, a very large step out of their cocoon. The first area of discomfort is obviously mental, to motivate oneself from laziness to taking exercise. Secondly, starting to take exercise causes some pain or at least physical discomfort.

We are superior to all other animals but we must contemplate what it is that makes us different. True, we have superior intelligence in that we can adapt to our environment and that we can learn from experiences. But do we? True, also, that we can think and reason. But do we use reason or are we controlled by our thoughts?

51 On being human

William James said that human nature is a combination of blind instinct and rational thought controlling or suppressing blind instinct. Herein lies the great conflict both personal and inter-personal.

This suppression of instincts, emotions, dreams and of self-expression begins at a very early age in childhood, in other words the roots of creativity are suppressed in the early stages of life.

What is the advantage of being human? It is the use of thought to be fulfilled and creative and to acknowledge and develop our spirituality. In other words to be happy.

52 Goals for achieving happiness

> First, CLEAR OUT YOUR MIND as discussed earlier. A psychoanalyst will tell you that a period of analysis will change your outlook on life, and you will discover many new things about yourself and hidden abilities. It is possible to do much 'soul searching' yourself in periods of contemplation so that you have a far greater understanding of self.
>
> One needs to have periods of SOLITUDE each day. Periods of time spent quietly and alone. This could be sitting alone at home, having a drink after work, or just in the car driving. It could be walking the dogs or in a church. Not many people spend time alone even in their holidays. It is as if they are afraid of the time alone and of their own thoughts.
>
> FITNESS. To be fit you should take at least three periods of 30 minutes aerobic exercise each week. Many people get their exercise at work running up stairs, others walking the dog or playing golf –

although for some people this may not be enough.

Strenuous exercise would appear to be essential to tune the body in the way it was intended. During strenuous exercise the body's own 'drugs' – endorphins are produced to sooth and relax the body and mind. The mind thrives on aerobic exercise. The cardiovascular system improves in efficiency. The pounding of feet on the ground must send the most basic of messages to the brain satisfying the instinct of hunting, thus providing fulfilment. The stimulation of proprioceptors in all of the body must give similar messages.

IN THIS MODE THE BODY AND MIND CAN BEST APPRECIATE NATURE. The smell of the rain or a freshly ploughed field or of newly cut grass. The sounds the hedgerows and the skies. The subtle differences in colour. The beauty of changing seasons and the daily changes of landscape, and the bliss of every type of weather from the bright crispiness of frost to the stinging of hailstones. The challenge of the winds to the refreshing rain as well as the beauty of a summer's day.

What you are doing here is going back to what is instinctive in your nature and creating an environment in which you can think unhindered by negative thoughts.

In this state the mind can be incredibly creative. Where ideas and solutions will simply flow in the most amazing way.

53 On running

One way to combine strenuous exercise and solitude is in running. I do not recommend it as being superior to any other way that you may choose. You may choose to exercise with others and have separate periods of solitude.

I think of my daily run as resembling every project in life, big or small. Firstly, it must be prepared for with food and liquid and time given for them to be digested into useful nourishment and not carried in the stomach as excess baggage.

A run must fit in with body rhythm and is best not done at different times each day unless practised for. There are similar good times and bad times in a day for important meetings so it is important to understand your body rhythms.

A satisfying run will be testing and therefore it requires motivation to undertake it and the assistance of visualization before setting out. I always visualize the turning point for home before I set out, and during the run I motivate myself, when I tire, by visualizing completing the journey without a stop.

On a testing run there will be hills. Often on the way up a hill there is a great urge to stop (there are many hills in life). It is important never to make a decision on the way up a hill always focus beyond the top. To stop on a hill sets a great psychological challenge for the next time you face that hill.

There is an interesting point here that I will come back to later. If you can relax and be distracted in thought then the hill will not be noticeable at all. However, there are many times that intense determination and concentration will be required to keep going before once again visualizing the finish or the turning point.

After a period of motivation and concentration comes a period of exhilaration and relaxation when no obstacle is insurmountable and in fact one is not aware of effort or even self. If you are properly prepared your body will help you in every task, assisted by the release of endorphines.

Eventually, tiredness will bring you back to consciousness and it may be time to turn for home. Tiredness and pain are, however, not important in this endeavour because by visualization and motivation and disassociation one can overcome them easily. Sometimes, when I take the run for granted, pain or tiredness will almost take over, it is like a voice within saying: 'Stop, spoil yourself – have a little rest.'

The problem is that if you give in once to discomfort you have re-defined the limits of the cocoon for that day because when the same level of discomfort is reached again you will not be able to resist the urge to stop. The beauty of my running is that it is done alone, and therefore there is no competition with anyone. This is the first big plus for me. It is very difficult not to compete with many things, to try to prove something. This must be resisted. I find the urge to pass a pedestrian before they reach a certain point or to race a cyclist up a hill, because I still have not come to terms with certain things.

Good and generous runners who pass me slow down for a while so that I do not feel bad because I am slower.

The second great advantage is the solitude. A time to think and a time to let many things run through my mind. It is remarkable how the solutions just flow. Many times at the end of a run I go immediately and write down my thoughts and ideas that just seem to come as flashes from nowhere.

There comes a time in every run to turn for home. Having climbed many hills there are obvious compensations in coming back down but this still takes effort and one must not be complacent. A different set of muscles is required and the same distance is to be covered although it always seems shorter.

Visualization and motivation are needed throughout. Each time pain or tiredness takes over a period of self-talk is the most comforting thing, such as reciting to yourself all those things you are good at. Do not be ashamed of them no-one can hear you. You will have a great feeling of inner warmth.

Regardless of what the weather is like, I enjoy everything that our climate produces. This is a wonderful by-product of my running. While other people moan about the weather the rain and the wind or the snow, I just cannot wait to run in it. So I am not depressed at being 'cheated' by our climate – I love it.

◇

54 Running lessons for life

There are many very important lessons from this simple daily run for everyday life.

1) Over the last 12 years I have run over 25,000 miles. If I thought on day one that I had 25,000 miles to do I would never have started, but they were done one at a time and each one brought challenge, enjoyment and satisfaction.
2) Never make a decision going up a hill except to keep on trying, but it is better and easier to be well prepared and relaxed with a clear vision of where you are going.
3) Strenuous exercise is a superb way to relieve stress and it is only by relaxing that the mind will be free to be productive or creative.
4) The only person worth competing against is yourself and that is best done not by forcing or trying, but by motivation and relaxation and visualization and some unashamed self-praising self-talk.
5) If you stop on a hill or when faced with a challenge this will become an even greater challenge next time it is confronted. If you need to stop on a hill it is important to set a

positive frame of mind first. You may need to stop on this occasion because of lack of food or general fatigue. Have a reason so that the next time, this hill will not force you to stop again. Your excuse may just be that you wish to spoil yourself today but promise effort tomorrow. Similarly, if a run is extended by an extra mile or two then that new distance becomes the new psychological barrier in future – pushing out the boundaries of the cocoon. It is the same in every aspect of life.

6) Many times when I run in the evening with a low sun behind me or at night with a car with full headlights behind me, I am conscious that the other driver in the oncoming car cannot see me. Similarly in life, you must accept that others have problems. Take this into account.

7) Pain is an unimportant thing. There is no need to tell anyone about it. Unless it is to a doctor.

8) Strenuous exercise improves the circulatory system. I have reduced my heart rate from over 80 beats per minute to 42. A massive improvement in efficiency. So when others are getting stressed and their heart rate is up to 100 or 120 mine is to 60 or maybe 80. Who will cope better?

55 Peace of mind

Most of the 25,000 miles that I have run in the last 12 years have been on the same stretch of road. I know every bump and hollow, each patch of grass. My body through normal regeneration has renewed itself perhaps 12 times as I run here.

I have lost approximately five pounds for every 10 miles along the way. That is over five tons of me is spread along the route.

Atoms that once were me are now in the grass, in the flowers, in the trees and in the animals. My 'new' body is made of atoms that I have breathed and swallowed as I ran.

Time always seems to stand still as I run: periods of solitude where time stands still. Does time only exist when you measure it?

We seek routine in our lives yet we are relaxed most when we break free of these routines for a while.

In the mind there is a freedom to go anywhere and to do anything. When I run my mind may be here at my desk writing, or visualizing me out there running. I can, as it were, be 'out of the body' watching myself.

In the most unpleasant situations it is possible to do the same thing. Have a happy peaceful place where you can go in your mind. Somewhere you would not spoil by taking stress and depression with you. Somewhere you know intimately that is filled with extremely pleasant memories. This could be somewhere you found while searching through your life.

Go there in your mind and find the peace and the re-invigoration that is always there.

I have enthused at length about the joys and benefits of running. These are the joys and benefits of strenuous exercise and solitude whatever way you choose to enjoy them, but they are essential for relaxation and clear thinking.

[*Deepak Chopra gave great meaning to these thoughts.*]

56 On success

You must learn that success comes from a relaxed mind. Our best results do not necessarily come from competition. We must compete in races to understand the environment of dealing with others who have similar goals to ourselves, but such competition may produce stress which will affect free flow in performance. So the only real competition should come from within, competing with yourself to control stress and to relax, to allow your best performance to take place. If preparation is done properly in every way the best – your best – will follow.

So the 'hills' of life are challenges only to your thoughts. Your thoughts will get you to the top of the hill or they will stop you. You control your thoughts. Remember also that coming downhill requires effort as well and a different set of muscles so this must be prepared for. The journey is never over until the end, and requires thought control and motivation at various stages all along the way.

◇

57 On nourishing the mind

Just as the body requires fluid and nourishment, the mind needs its nourishment also.

If one takes only one type of exercise muscles are inclined to tighten and ache. Similarly with the mind: it is essential to have more than one interest so that a change can relax the tensions that will build up, even in people with good control over their thoughts.

I have often thought that companies should use their workforce in different departments that bear no obvious relationship to each other to help relax the mind and encourage a free flow of new ideas. For example; moving staff a few at a time from the accounts to the legal department, may bring about a better trained and more flexible, relaxed and therefore more productive workforce. Of course, if they were encouraged to be fit, perhaps with exercise as part of the daily routine and also solitude, then a very fulfilled and productive workforce would emerge.

58 On trying to impress

Do things only for yourself not to impress others. Whether or not you try to impress, people will ultimately make up their own minds about you. If you are good at something they will notice. If you tell them you are good you are asking for a judgement. You will then have to try to live up to the expectations you have created. Now you are trying to do things, so you are breaching one of the fundamental rules and it will therefore interfere with the natural flow of your creativity, you will also become tired more quickly.

I have often said that I perform best when in a moment of crisis. When my back is to the wall. This would seem to contradict what I have just said. But it does not really breach the rules. At times like this you are not trying to impress others but are singlemindedly focused on a challenge and drawing deep on inner resources, so creating a good environment for the flow of ideas.

Nature also gives us a basic protective instinct and therefore at times like this will give the extra energy to carry on, twenty-four hours a day if necessary. However, effort is involved here and the body and mind will tire. This cannot be sustained for long periods.

You must know and believe that there are almost no boundaries to the resourcefulness of your body and mind as long as you are prepared to go beyond your comfort cocoon.

59 On individual qualities

There is another point worth emphasizing here. That is that having accepted that we have individual qualities, we must have confidence in those abilities to advance ourselves by utilizing them.

I watched an interesting programme the other day with my children; it was a cartoon called 'Rug Rats' which is about very young children and babies playing together. The episode I watched centred around one of the children named Chuckie who had an imaginary friend with whom he played while alone.

I am sure most people have seen children play like this when alone. The other children observed him and when he told them how super this friend was they all wanted to play.

Eventually, but reluctantly, he agreed. They had many days of great fun playing together. Playing games thought up by this invisible person who spoke through Chuckie.

However, as the days went by the games became more adventurous to the point of danger to the young children. Chuckie became concerned and withdrew his friend. The following day they all sat depressed, unable to think of anything to do or to play. Their inspiration was gone. Even Chuckie could not think of anything that interested the others or indeed himself.

The programme raised some rather interesting ideas: the concept of leadership and religion. It demonstrated that if you believe and trust completely in somebody then you are happy for them to rule your life. It showed also that when we do not accept total responsibility for our own actions life appears more comfortable because we have someone else to rely on, someone else to make our decisions for us and someone else to take the blame if it goes wrong. However, all the time the comfort zone constricts and the inclination or the ability to think for one's self becomes increasingly difficult.

It showed also that it is difficult for many people to realize that their own ideas, their own thoughts, are worthwhile and that they have a value.

I will return to this very simple story later because it so clearly demonstrates the need for self-confidence and the need to take control of ones own life.

60 On bravery

We hear stories so often of how people acted with great bravery and courage in the face of most horrific situations because there was no time to process the situation and to interpret it in the terms of self. In these situations people act in an unexpected way – unexpected to themselves, and after it is over they collapse and cry and marvel at what they have done.

While there was an emergency they acted like the virtuoso pianist who plays straight from his subconscious to his fingers – they instinctively knew what to do and did it.

When people are asked how they feel after a death or a great loss, or after a great achievement, they will commonly reply that they need time for events to sink in. There is no immediate emotion.

Having assimilated the event there will follow many feelings and emotions. Emotion is how you handle the experience, how you 'season' it with all past experiences.

61. On exploring our potential

There are completely unexplored areas in most of us; greater resources than we may ever know. These are the resources that people only discover when their life is in danger. We hear people who speak of the great strength that enabled them to pick the car up to protect somebody in an accident, or how they found great resources to save people from a tragedy or in a fire.

It would seem that there is perhaps another gear or many other gears that we can change into in our everyday lives if we can only tap into these resources. The resources that we often demonstrate exist.

It should give us great confidence in our own

abilities to know that we have this deep inner strength to carry on even when our body is screaming at us to stop.

If we watch children playing we will see that they have boundless energy. When they are doing something that they enjoy they will carry on literally until they drop to sleep. Similarly, we have tremendous energy when we are pursuing the things that we enjoy doing.

For example, if you were playing a very strenuous game of squash, no matter how tired you are as soon as the ball begins to move you move along with it. You do not think about the difficulty in breathing, the pain or the damage to the injury that you incurred earlier. That ball is moving. There is no pain just effort and pleasure.

When the ball stops again you realize how tired you have been. But if that game was a chore and you were doing it to impress somebody else, or they were forcing you to carry on, then you would feel the tiredness and the game would suffer because of it.

So it is only in being relaxed and being motivated from within rather than by outside forces that we can carry on to live our full potential.

62 Expressing emotions

We talked earlier of how we found it difficult to share the most profound emotions of others.

We find it equally difficult to express our own feelings. To borrow the words from the Carpenters' song: 'We tried to talk it over but the words got in the way.' We have often heard people say: 'There are no words to express how I feel.'

We have a language of many thousands of words yet it so often fails us on these occasions. Only a very few gifted people and artistic giants have been able to express their feelings in a way which enables us to empathize with them. This is through music and art and fewer still through words.

Because we do not have such powers we should never not attempt to express ourselves. Such attempts can be both a regenerative and mutually rewarding experience at a different level.

◇

63 On relaxation and visualization

Before one can practise concentration, visualization or regression, one must learn how to relax.

The basic routine for relaxing which has been repeated in many books is simply to sit or preferably to lie, comfortably in pleasant surroundings. When relaxed, start to identify each muscle group in an orderly fashion in the body starting with the feet or the head or the hands, and to tense each muscle group and then relax up gradually through each limb through the body, through the neck and shoulders to the jaws and face. Tensing and relaxing so that all the tension is gone from the body.

Try to feel as if you are floating off the bed. Feel that there is no pressure between any part of your body and the bed. Then as you relax breathe slowly and deeply and as you exhale through your nose feel as if you are inflating your body. Feel as if you are blowing air through your body and that you are inflating gently like a balloon to help you to float off the surface on which you are lying.

In relaxing it is important also to control self-talk. Having relaxed, chase all thoughts from your mind. Do not dwell on anything. This should be done as a relaxing exercise, so do not be concerned about the thoughts which will keep coming. Just gently chase them away.

Having cleared the mind of all unwanted thoughts start to dwell on a particular point of interest. This may be something that you wish to achieve, for example winning a race, or passing an exam. Begin to picture yourself having achieved what you most want. Picture yourself winning the race or receiving the diploma. Build this picture in every detail try to hear the sounds, try to smell the environment, try to sense with all of your senses. Dwell in this state of satisfaction of having achieved your wish. Practise this exercise many times for everything that you wish to achieve.

Use this exercise to picture the new you that you want to achieve now that you have the will to change.

64 On self-expression

I saw a fascinating programme on television recently about the history of the sub four-minute mile.

All the athletes involved were without doubt highly motivated individuals. Yet they expressed the motivation in very different ways.

Roger Bannister spoke of dissociating his mind from his aching body. It was as if his body was not part of him as he ran. Ryun spoke of his running as a religious experience and spoke of his relationship with God and of God speaking to him and sending him messages.

Sebastian Coe and Steve Ovett have yet different ways of addressing this very personal experience. Steve Cram had an even more relaxed 'facade' to his great efforts.

Bannister presented a clear picture of what can be achieved through self-belief and motivation in a way that one would want to explore more. The deeply religious expressions of Ryun would not evoke in me the same feelings.

Adam Smith addressed this problem in his 'Theory of Moral Sentiments' when he spoke of how it was easy to share the emotion of joy with a friend in his good fortune. And to feel with him his sadness for his great loss. To feel also his anger and share his anger for his enemy.

Though we cannot feel or even come close to feeling the deep love that our friend experiences for his mate. That love that drives him to right soppy poetry strikes us as amusing.

Likewise, many cannot share in the deep religious feelings enjoyed by others.

Love is where there is no judgement or manipulation; just harmony in chemistry and in all interactions. When you have this synergy then you can express the real you.

◇

65 The principle of communication

We also said earlier that we react based on past experiences and we try to communicate based on mutual past experiences with others. You may say:
'I feel like there is a ton weight on my shoulders.'
'I feel like I am being pulled in four different directions at once.'

If you try to describe an orange to a blind person who had no experience of fruit before, where would you start? But if that person had seen a lemon before going blind your job would be so much easier.

We communicate by simile and metaphor and by analogy.

This book tries to make its point many times by analogy: 'YOU PLC', 'You as a derelict building', 'Your clearing in the jungle'.

Julian Jaynes in his book on the origins of consciousness makes the argument that the very origin of words is in metaphor, that early man built his vocabulary by combining his limited repertoire of sounds to make new sounds, 'words', to describe things. Why then do we speak, and by being able to speak have we lost other forms of communication that would have been more reliable; for example, telepathy and body language?

Have you ever observed the enormous flocks of birds that are commonly seen over the sea or the countryside? They swoop and climb and dive in harmony as if they were a cloud with a single mind.

Groups of mammals are similarly inclined to respond and move together, certainly amongst the more advanced, such as apes, by body language.

We speak to communicate. We communicate to find common ground with others. We communicate also with others to express our needs from society and to express our fears. We communicate to try to show that we are not a threat to others.

We obviously have to take account of all the fears and needs of others. But we now know that other people cannot always express themselves well and situations are quite often made worse, much worse, by saying too much.

We have a communication problem at all levels in human relationships. From husband with wife to nation with nation. All of these problems are due to a failure to understand self in a totally honest way.

66 More reflections on self-talk and control of our thoughts

The words that we use to communicate with others we also use in our head, and, as we have seen [Section 9], we call this our SELF-TALK. If there were no words would you be able to think? What would replace your self-talk? Would your thinking be purer and quicker or would it be uncontrolled and lead to your destruction?

We need our language to help to coordinate our memories. Our memories are not stored in words but as chemical bytes which produce auras

Self-talk helps us to programme our mind and re-programme it. In its purest form self-talk would also be the words that get in the way.

But this could only be the case if all the bad programming had ben changed so that a flow from the subconscious would be perfection.

There are no words in your periods of

solitude when your mind is 'somewhere else'. Perhaps at these times your mind is being bathed in chemical pictures and auras from your memory. We call this a day-dream, a pleasurable wallow in the chemistry of the mind.

No-one ever mentions a 'daymare' – the day dream equivalent to a nightmare. We might describe a 'daymare', therefore, as when self-talk is provoking a sequence of memories of unpleasant experiences causing guilt and worry and anxiety.

The intrusion of self-talk on mental activity can be controlled by concentration. As noted earlier, the conscious mind is capable of doing only one task at a time. If it is occupied with useless and damaging self-talk it will not be possible to think clearly.

To learn to concentrate it is essential to focus on only one thing and to exclude all other intrusions. You can practise for this by setting aside a period of quiet each day when you chase all thoughts from your mind. Refuse to dwell on anything. Learn to have a completely clear screen. I will return to this later.

For solitude you need quiet, from without and from within.

67 Personal space and 'the clearing of the jungle'

From the very beginning of time man has set boundaries and limitations on himself. We still do. We like to maintain our own personal space in encounters – an area around us into which no-one is welcome except our more intimate friends and relations.

In encounters we invite people into this space by handshakes and other bodily contact, for example by kissing when we meet someone. We also send a signal by not inviting people to breach this space on meeting them.

Our next area of personal territory is our home and within that home we each have our own personal space. There are times when we seek privacy within the home. Beyond the home there is our street and our district and our country.

We also live in social groups. This group may be limited to family. There may be slightly larger groups associated with work or hobbies. A group of 30 or less seems to be about the average number suitable for most people to be comfortable to socialize in.

All of these physical boundaries that man requires are natural and important. But the mental boundaries and limitations that he places on himself, while they may be natural to animals, are not natural to intelligent man.

68 | The survival instinct

Early man in the jungle will have lived in a small social group and not strayed much from outside the boundaries of his clearing – his village. Beyond his clearing was the unknown, the threat to his survival.

The instinct for survival will always dominate over all. In terms of survival of the fittest, those who were not concerned for their own survival are dead; cautious man survived and we are his descendants.

We are therefore instinctively careful. Even a very young child has a fear of noise. Indeed all animals react defensively to noise. It is easy to understand the reaction of primitive man, therefore, to the noises of the jungle beyond his village. The sounds of the jungle animals and the noises of the storms and the thunder coupled with the visible and tangible effects of the elements, will have caused great fear.

As the child grew in these surroundings he heard these noises and observed the effects on the adults. The reactions of the adults became ingrained in his subconscious.

Fear grew with the imagination of a great and powerful being out there who controlled the elements and used them to rebuke man.

Man began to seek mercy from this powerful being. He would offer to give up those things that were most important to him in exchange for peace. Eventually, altars were built and sacrifices made to appease the gods. These rituals became established and handed down over the generations to become the precursors of organized religion. To breach these rituals caused great guilt. In the primitive mind, if the storm blew or the lightning struck man was guilty in some way or another.

So man prayed to the gods to be allowed to survive. He was no longer able to survive on his own, but only by the permission of the gods. Only by their permission would his crops grow, or would he find the energy or the ability to look after himself. In his mind he was of no worth in himself.

We are now back to the simple story in the 'Rug Rats'.

Now spend a little time thinking of the analogy to your own talents of what you have just been reading. You have worth in yourself and no boundaries.

69 On giving yourself credit

We have just been talking about a man living in the Stone Age and surviving where modern man would most likely die. Stone Age man was very resourceful: he made his own implements, built his shelter, made his clothes, and brought up his family against what, in our terms, would be all the odds. But he gave credit for his very existence to another.

It is very easy to understand the fears of Stone Age man and to imagine the absolute darkness at night with only the eery light and shadows given from the flickering of a fire onto the trees around him. The noises of the jungle must have caused a feeling of terror at times as they would to many of us today even with our knowledge and understanding of their cause.

How many people today are uncomfortable to be alone in their own houses? Today people live with irrational fears in all areas of life and suffer crippling guilt needlessly, just like primitive man. Like him, but thousands of years later, some people still do not have any understanding of their own resourcefulness and talents.

People too readily put themselves down and give credit for their success to others. Each individual has similarly remarkable talents for survival. If you were stranded on a desert island you would 'instinctively' survive. You would build a shelter, make a fire, find your food and protect yourself. This resourcefulness would come from within with all actions done only for you, not to impress anyone.

70 | On setting limits on ourselves

In many such circumstances, in self-talk, people will have conversations with an imaginary friend whom they will ask for help and guidance and to whom they will give credit for their success.

Whatever is bad in their lives they attribute to the spirit of evil, and whatever is good is attributed to the spirit of goodness.

So out of instinct, out of fear and guilt, and out of our failure to acknowledge our own resourcefulness we have moved into our mental cocoon, and left our futures to be decided by others. In other words, our own self-limiting powers have set up this cocoon in our subconscious.

Once again we are coming back to the simple message of the 'Rug Rats'.

This clearing in the jungle of early man represents our mental cocoon, and his physical boundaries represent our self-imposed limits expressed in 'I cannot do it'.

Throughout history we have held in awe those who endeavoured to push beyond those barriers: the explorers, the athletes, the astronauts. Consider how we have lavished honours and wealth upon them. We have, by association with them, gone beyond our own limitations.

<>

71 On giving

But it is easily seen that the boundaries of the jungle clearing are arbitrary and they can be extended without limits, as long as the interests of others are respected along the way. The boundaries can be pushed to the edges of the continent and then beyond by simply addressing a new set of challenges. There is an interesting thought here. As society grew and man became more confident he outgrew the guilt which controlled him. This appears to be happening today. Is this why civilizations have collapsed?

If man is not controlled by guilt must this always lead to the expression of all his selfish weakness?

How will it be possible to have everyone understand that the GREATEST JOY AND SELF-SATISFACTION IS IN GIVING NOT TAKING?

The religions which evolved from the primitive gods, for example, the Catholic religion, controlled by guilt while trying to teach this message of altruism. But the teaching was that we are of little worth in ourselves and that we must spend our life in preparation for something and someone better; a selfish goal. This would seem to be a misrepresentation of Christianity.

LIFE IS NOT A DRESS REHEARSAL. Life must be enjoyed, therefore, without guilt or self-limitations. However, you cannot ignore the spiritual side of your existence – that imaginary strand that attaches you to all like-minded people. Is this your contact with the life you will have once you have had your journey in the body?

72 On our individuality

Each of us is special because we are all individuals with our own combination of talents unlike anybody else. We have our own ability and our own way of doing things. If two people were to play a solo instrument in a concerto they would play the same piece of music differently.

No two people are the same. So even if your talents do seem the same as other people your approach will be individual. You have something to contribute in life. This is the important thing because it is not what you get out of life that makes it successful; it is what you put in.

When you think of all those that we regard as successful: the performers, the sportsmen, those who have made far more money than they will ever have need for, they still carry on performing because they wish to push out their personal boundaries a little bit further to see how far they can go.

Perhaps there are some external motivating factors of praise, of awards, of applause, of adoration. All of these are the wrong reasons for doing anything. These are the pay-offs that some people become hooked upon.

73. The right to succeed

There are many who feel they do not have any right to succeed; success is for others. They feel that their role is the worker not the leader. Not every man can or must be a leader. But you are the leader of your own mind and that is all that is important.

So you start to make preparations to move out, to stretch your boundaries and to explore. The important part of your preparation is thought. Thought in preparation is very important because what you believe firmly will become a reality.

◇

74. On the fear of failure

One of the great restraints of success is the fear of failure. You have often heard that it is not important whether you win or lose, just how you have played the game. This is very true. Often enough at school, whether it be to do with games or academic/artistic achievement, there will be two very talented people in the same group; typically, one will score better than the other even though they both gave of their best. One can never be a failure in these circumstances.

What is important is not the winning, because there is an important lesson in the failure. If you have done your preparation properly you will be satisfied with how you played the game. You must look on not having achieved the result as a valuable learning experience, and you must emerge from that encounter fulfilled. If you have given of your best winning is secondary.

Thomas Edison who invented the electric light bulb experimented, it is said, over 10,000 times before he finally had success. He was interviewed after his success and asked how he managed to carry on when he had failed so often. He is reported to have replied: 'I have not failed. What I have learned is 10,000 ways that do not work.'

So having planned and thought out your plan of your future of your journey beyond this clearing, having got your body in order and your mind in order, having taken with you what you need for the journey, then your approach must be single-minded, and single-minded only for the present.

75 On the past

What has happened before while you lived in the clearing, the rows and disagreements that you have had with others, the fights, the jealousy, whether or not someone had taken your wife, or whether or not someone had abused you or hurt you or been offensive to you, is not significant for your journey in the future.

All of those things from the past are left

behind you in the clearing and you have learned from each one of them, you have accepted them and come to terms with each of them. Likewise, what is beyond is not to be worried about because worry is preoccupying the present with what might or might not happen in the future. The future is under your control, but you are living today not the future.

What you do today is a preparation for your future.

76 On dealing with others

As you move into new territory you must not take anything for granted. You do not know what kind of dangers lie ahead, so you must be on your guard. You must be alert, but your intelligence, your cunning and your instincts will guide you because you have planned.

This is where the time spent in contemplation, absorbing useful material into your mind will help you. There will be times when your instinct may be to withdraw, but this is not failure – this is positive action – to withdraw and re-group and move forward again.

Always think ahead, move forward and any withdrawal is part of your forward plan. As you move out from your clearing you may happen upon another clearing with other people there. These other people may not be as in control of their fears, they may not be as trusting, they may not be as relaxed as you are and therefore this encounter could go very wrong or to your advantage.

You cannot leave this encounter to be controlled by the other people. You must not abdicate any control. You must handle this encounter and handle it on your terms – on terms of friendship – on trust.

You must communicate while appreciating the problems of the other person. If you are driving down the road and a car approaches you on a narrow country road with its head-lights full on, do you put on your head-lights as well so that you can blind him just as he is blinding you so that you both crash into each other and die? You do not. In this situation you may indicate that he is posing a difficulty and then you will stop and pull over. Obviously this saves him but more importantly it saves you.

So when as you make these journeys you encounter others who are at a disadvantage. It is important to take on board what their problems are, and actually say to them: 'I understand your problem. It is entirely possible to rid yourself of these problems and I can help you to do that so that life can be better for both of us.'

How many times in everyday life do situations like this arise? How many human encounters can be turned into happy occasions just simply with this thought, even though hostilities are coming from the other party. If hostility is met with hostility there is a very rapid downward spiral with negative responses back and forth. However, one positive response can upset the downward spiral and turn it back upwards again or at worst, with positive responses, this situation can be turned onto a plateau until such time as the other party may also react in a positive way. Then it begins to spiral upwards again.

77 On embracing the whole world

The whole quest, therefore, is a pursuit of happiness, of peace of mind and that is gained by making the whole world your territory and embracing it, by having no bounds, no limits to any area of your existence, be it in your mind or in your body. There is no happiness any other way. And having such happiness we can pass it on to others.

This is a journey that you make alone, a journey of the mind. It is a personal journey and there will be times when you need to re-motivate yourself.

When you are up against a challenge you will need to concentrate and motivate yourself to move forward.

Remember it is important psychologically never to stop on the way up the hill unless you do so in the right frame of mind. Remember also there is no failure as long as having an undesired outcome is approached in the right frame of mind.

78 On our spirituality

Let us think again about the invisible friend in the 'Rug-Rats'. It is good to have the invisible friend along with you – someone you can talk to, someone you can ask for help. Herein lies what I believe to be God. As I suggested earlier, I believe that God is a focal point of all good thought, of all the good wishes for other people, for example, when many people come together and pray (they do not have to come together in the same building). If a strand was attached from each one of those people as they wished each other well, the union of all those strands, the focus of all that thought must be God.

So that while we are on our journey and while we are in a perfect frame of mind; while we wish everyone else well and try in every encounter to see the best in everybody then we are with God.

We see many people who go into a church and kneel and pray for hours on end and then come out and continue their life of causing trouble and anxiety for others, sometimes even immediately after they leave the church. That may be religion but it is not about God because it is not about goodness.

79 We are not alone

We can stop and plug in at any time to this communication with others of goodwill and ask for help. You are not alone on your journey. This can be the invisible friend in your mind, a friend that is all goodness. I firmly believe that this is the case.

So many young people today are growing up with no teaching in schools of anything to do with the spiritual side of our being. I often wonder where do they go in their mind when they seek help. Are we doing a great disservice to our younger generations by not teaching them to seek out the spiritual side of their being?

Once you have spent some time exploring your own mind and coming to terms with all the negativity, and when you have become positive and motivated not for any external reasons, not to impress but simply for happiness; the happiness that comes with achievement; the happiness that comes with knowing that you are getting the best from yourself and from life: you will also come to appreciate that there must be a spiritual side to our being and that it is there to help all of us.

◇

80 On dreams

Some nights, instead of a comforting relaxing night's sleep, one has a nightmare or at least awakens with the awareness of having been dreaming; of having a disturbed night.

This is the same process (of deliberating) taking place. The subconscious is chewing over all of the happenings of the previous day. It is chewing over all of the information that has been collected. It is also chewing over the input of information for the following day and of plans for the future. As the information is assimilated it is played against similar experiences from the past, and the particular experience is matched to the closest such past experience.

In these situations you may have been happy or sad, in control or totally out of control. You may be a child in an adult environment. You may have been under threat or not. And so on.

Some of these memories may, as they are brought together out of many different contexts in your past, form a nightmare or a dream, in the surreal way that dreams occur. A pageant of flashes from occasions when you felt as you did in today's experience.

Sometimes the dream will not be recalled when you waken but you will waken feeling happy and encouraged or you may waken feeling angry or anxious or just depressed. These moods are a hangover from the dreams of the night before.

On other occasions we get the feeling of *déjà vu* as the anticipated experience, from the dreams, occurs as we are involved in some particular activity.

On yet other occasions we can recall a dream during the next day and recall the mood we felt at that time. This may come as a feeling of a certain mood and then, suddenly, a recall of the dream. Sometimes, we find it hard to shake off that mood.

This once again re-enforces the argument that you can control your mood by placing the correct information in the subconscious mind.

81 The journey to work

A point was raised much earlier in the book as to why you feel the way you do today.

As we look at that question again, perhaps many of the answers now come more easily.

Did you dream last night? Try to remember the dream and then try to discover the circumstances at present in your life that provoked it. Why does the subconscious in registering this episode evoke the particular set of emotions in your dream?

Play the dream back to help you to understand your present emotions. It may also help in decision-making today.

Have you got anxieties about the day or the future? Look at all the things that cause you anguish and see if they can be made less threatening. We have discussed the procedure for eliminating worry.

There is no joy in not facing problems. This just leads to shrinking the comfort zone. It enforces fear. Confronting problems eliminates the negative chemistry.

Strive to take the stress out of situations. Bring forward those issues about which you are anxious. Is guilt or worry bothering you, if so sit down and write out your problems as discussed.

Is someone else causing you worry, or causing you problems? 'Are their headlights in your eyes?' If so raising your headlight will not help. Try to warn the offender. If they do not comply do not fight. Pull over and let them by – at least in most cases. Seek ways to reduce stress.

On your way to work stop and let people out of the side roads. Stop and let children cross the road. Your children are out there somewhere too. Say a hearty good morning to everyone when you arrive at work. Give unexpected gifts. Telephone people or go to them to tell them how good they are at their job. Do you like praise, do you like sympathy? So do they.

Do something special to please another no matter how small and see how it makes you feel good. It is almost unjust that we get so great a reward for being nice to people.

If you are having an unpleasant encounter how are you seasoning it? Declare your interests to yourself with honesty in every situation.

Use self-talk to remotivate yourself when you

are feeling down. Check your posture is it the posture of someone happy, if not change it.

The single most useful way to eliminate some stress from a busy life is to make lists of all you wish to do each day. I keep a large notebook with a never-ending list which is continually updated. When everything is on the list, the most important things stand out, and the mind is not burdened trying to remember.

◇

82 Who are you?

Having pondered much through the first part of this book about the advantages of change and the person you would like to be, it is worthwhile at this stage to look again at the starting point. Who *you* are. It will be very easy to understand the need for change and to see the way forward if *you* know and accept the *you* of the present. We have spent much time talking about and trying to understand how *you* became the way *you* are, what forces were involved and how they had their effect.

Are you the physical presence as observed by others? This is not possible because tall people will call you normal or small, small people will call you tall. Fat people and thin people similarly. Some will find you aggressive, whilst others will find you calming. Some may call you dumb while others will consider you bright and so on.

As we saw earlier, we all play a role in

every encounter, we may play the role of a parent to parent or a parent to child, or of siblings and equals. Each encounter is further complicated by the male-to-male relationship or the male-to-female relationship or the female-to-female relationship.

◇

83 On judging others

People's views of others are also unfortunately affected by race, colour and disabilities. So you are not the physical presence.

The physical presence is judged by others according to their standards, their problems, their inadequacies and their prejudices. To be aware of the difficulties caused in our lives by the judgements of us by other people we only need to reflect on how often we have to say that a person has misunderstood us, misunderstood our intentions and have got the situation completely wrong, to understand that the real you is not just the physical presence.

You at present have similar difficulties in judging others. Many of these judgements are made in first 30 seconds of an encounter whilst there is leakage of body language – as we discussed earlier.

In each encounter in the first few seconds you tell others how to judge you by leakage from your subconscious through body language. But you would proclaim immediately on watching a video of yourself that this is not the real you, that you are not really like this and this most certainly is not the person you wish to be or to project.

◇

84. On others judging us

So we have a situation where it is accepted that we do not accept the judgements of us by others. *So the physical presence is not you.*

It is also obvious that the leakage from the subconscious certainly does not portray the person that you would want to be either.

You will argue, therefore, that you wish to be different, you wish to be seen as different from the way you are judged at present. You may feel that if only people could read these thoughts they would find the real person. So is it possible that your conscious thoughts are the real you.

◇

85. On thought and the subconscious

Then we must ask what is thought?

Thought can be conscious or subconscious. The conscious mind is to the subconscious as the body is to the heart. While the body will tire and need rest the heart is made of a different type of muscle that does not rest in the same way. Yet the heart cannot survive without the body to provide for it. Of course the heart can be strained and over- worked or damaged by the lack of care. So can the subconscious mind.

The conscious mind similarly provides for the subconscious. It gathers information, assesses it and if it considers that information to be true or of value it passes it to the subconscious mind for action or for storage.

While the conscious mind will tire and need a rest, the subconscious mind like the heart continues to work.

You are at present the total of everything that you have thought to be true and valid so far in your life. All significant experiences have been stored in the subconscious.

Every experience of every day of your life has been stored in the subconscious mind. If you regress in your mind as we discussed before, you can go to any day in your life and re-live it. The more important emotional experiences will be the more easily remembered. Those very happy days or sad days, those episodes of embarrassment or guilt, of satisfaction or fulfilment will rush back easily.

If you were to go and sit with some old school friends or family then the memories will pour back very easily. So you can see that every day of your existence is recorded right from conception. It has been shown by recent research that every note of music that you have heard has been stored in the subconscious mind, and every episode of each day has been recorded likewise.

◇

86 How the mind works

Every baby is conceived with a mind like a computer which has no data in it. The baby cannot make judgements until it has something to compare experiences with. So its early experiences have to be accepted as true. No matter how wrong, how horrendous or how unjust these experiences may be they must be accepted as true and thus passed to the subconscious mind.

Further experiences will be judged against these experiences that have been accepted as true.

It will be many years before the child has reached 'the age of reason' but when this stage of life comes all of the reasoning is done against a background of all previous experiences.

So our thinking, our reasoning, our analysis of new situations is prejudiced by our previous experiences. Not only do we start our lives in the early years by recording wrong information, we then use that information to make a judgement on new experiences and record them as valid or not against that background. We continue throughout our lives to make wrong judgements and then to record those wrong judgements as true.

Therefore it is possible that a large percentage of the information recorded in our subconscious mind is wrong.

Since we accept that the conscious mind provides for the subconscious mind, it is controlled by the subconscious mind and is in many ways, therefore, working with false data. So, you could argue, the conscious mind is not you.

But the subconscious is not the real you either. We have said that you are the sum of all previous experiences. This is the present you, the you that is betrayed by body language, the you with which you are unhappy, the 'you' you wish to change.

The real you must be and can only be that blank computer on the day of conception with boundless potential.

87 The power of thought

It can only be from this perspective that the wish for change, the pursuit of perfection comes. It will come through the elimination of all that is untrue in your subconscious; the elimination of all that prejudices your perfect existence.

So how is this to be done. We have said that the subconscious mind will accept anything that the conscious mind holds as true.

Therefore you can change and correct the subconscious programming. This is done by the power of thought, conscious thought, which will nourish the subconscious which is the heart that beats through your mental existence.

The wish for change that comes from very deep within us comes with boundless potential. With that wish you can change all that you dislike about yourself, and having recorded it in the subconscious it will be subconsciously leaked to all those around you so that the real you will exist. The wish will become a reality in your subconscious, in your conscious and in your physical presence.

Not everything in your subconscious is wrong and some of the programming may just be slightly limiting. If you accept that everyone is similarly limited then certain limitations may even be endearing.

88 Discovering our excellence

Another important fact is that everyone has, just as they are right now, some area of excellence either latent or known.

If you have known abilities then the present state of the subconscious allows this excellence. But this can be developed further by removing much in the subconscious that must be limiting your ability.

While you are involved in your area of excellence i.e. practising your art, conscious thought need not be involved. For example, an artist or a sportsman or an author will describe it as a flow of inspiration.

Composers have attributed their work to the spiritual intervention of dead composers, authors have likewise felt that the work came from divine inspiration. Because they have struggled to understand how ideas can rush from their subconscious almost quicker than they can write.

Have you ever found that you have woken in the night with the solution to a problem that has bothered you for days? This is because in your sleep you are not thinking about the problem but in your subconscious all the information necessary for the decision has been assimilated, unhindered by conscious thought and the answer flows.

People who are senile and have lost all the power of concentration can have great recall of events past as their subconscious wanders through its memory banks unhindered by conscious distractions. They can recall in great clarity earlier periods of their lives but in no particular order. This demonstrates two points: firstly that episodes of our lives have been recorded and with great accuracy, and secondly that this information can be accessed.

89 On morning activity

It is accepted that the mind early in the morning is found to be very productive. It is a good time for study and for learning, it is also a good time for planning the day. This is because the conscious mind has been rested and can concentrate better, and that after a night's sleep the information of the previous day has been assimilated so that solutions are found easily and the future planned.

All successful men and women claim that to be successful one must rise early in the morning and set aside a period of contemplation in order to consider the day ahead. This period of contemplation makes it possible to tap into the night's deliberations of the unimpeded subconscious where solutions are to be found.

This period of time might be in solitude or walking the dog or taking exercise or just the journey alone to work.

◇

90 On moods and happiness

Earlier I re-stated the fact that you can betray your subconscious thoughts through body language. A very good example is your mood.

If you ask a child to draw a happy face or a sad face he would have no difficulty in doing so. Ask anyone to adopt a depressed posture or a confident posture or any other posture you may wish and they will do so at will.

Hypnosis has shown that a person cannot be happy while adopting a depressed posture and vice versa, but if allowed to change the posture they could immediately change their mood.

So it is obvious that you have to start telling yourself that you are happy, and believe that you possess whatever good qualities you wish to have for yourself before it happens. But it can happen in a second just by changing your mind.

While the subconscious is the heart of the mind, it is nourished by the conscious mind and the desire to change the conscious mind comes from the real you. The real you is that untainted vestige of your mind at conception that retains the irrepressible desire for perfection and perfect self-expression in peaceful happiness. It is said that we use less than one per cent of the brain's capacity and therefore there is no shortage of potential for change.

You have a talent that can be purified to flow from you consistently and predictably. Relax and find it.

◇

91 On humour

Humour has the opposite effect to stress. A package of potent chemicals released instantly that gives you exhilaration and a happy state of mind. Humour will assist in decision-making for the same reasons.

By reducing stress and by treating the mind chemically, humour offers options in the way of looking at things.

A simple joke alters the stressful situation and will change depression because as well as its chemical help, it is a symbol of sharing which conflicts with the self-indulgence of depression.

In extreme tension people will often laugh hysterically for no apparent reason. It is a physically and emotionally draining exercise. 'We laughed until we could laugh no more', but we felt so good afterwards.

Use humour to help to relieve stress and depression. Also to help in decision-making.

☐ Laughter bonds.

☐ Laughter relieves tension and stress.

☐ Laughter relieves depression.

☐ Laughter helps in decision-making.

<>

92 On making meetings worthwhile

How do you use this information that you have been collecting about yourself? If you are to attend an interview or an important meeting, for example, at the bank to arrange a loan, or if you are to be involved in a public debate with someone, you would do a lot of preparation.

Firstly, you would gather all the necessary information and study it. You would find our what the other person requires of you. Then you would want to know about the other person, his likes and dislikes, his hobbies etc, so that you could have a positive and worthwhile conversation with this person and so strike up a rapport. In a very important matter you might need a psychologist's report on the person to highlight his strong points and his weak points and to glean any other useful information.

Almost everyone in the world of business has a superior to report to and impress. What do they require to fulfil this need? They need to file a report on the meeting. This report must contain all necessary information and you are obliged to supply this.

I know that each time I go to the bank that the manager is writing a report as we talk so I always prepare for the meeting in a way which facilitates his job.

> You cannot ask a professional, a friend or anyone to breach their code of morals or ethics and retain a good working relationship afterwards.

If I am to enter into a debate I always start by asking myself what arguments will the opposition use and then work to counter these points.

These are some of the considerations for everyday encounters but always remember that your opponent is doing the same with regard to you.

93 On the need for self-analysis

In all the books I have read about such matters I have never once seen an exhortation that one should spend as much time as possible on self-analysis.

Much time has been spent in this book talking about you, the real you, your worries, concerns, prejudices, phobias, stresses, and anxieties. All of which are affecting your judgement on every issue.

Your opponents are trying to pre-judge you and perhaps pay money to psychologists to analyse you from a distance. But only you know the real you hang-ups and all.

Or do you?

After much self-analysis you will have a great understanding of self. If you are truly honest with yourself. Only you know the hidden agenda and what feeds it. Why you react to situations the way you do. Why you react to different people the way you do. Are you motivated by money or by personal ambitions or by family ambitions?

Is race or creed even slightly affecting your judgement? You can be totally honest with yourself in your mind and you must be, to succeed. You must acknowledge all your emotions. You must acknowledge and admit to yourself how circumstances affect you. You must try in regression to understand why you feel this way.

You must now understand and acknowledge

what is influencing your judgement. Declare to yourself your interest. Ask yourself are you the best person to be involved in this meeting?

- How does the other person see you?
- What does he want from you?
- How would you react if you were he?
- How would he react if he was you?

Know your enemy or adversary or opponent. Know those from whom you require help or a favour but most importantly know yourself honestly.

◇

94 On making better decisions

Have all your decisions so far been good? If not how would you improve? You must first of all learn from your failures. So-called failures are lessons on how not to do something and are therefore very beneficial as long as they are seen in that way.

So, the question arises, why might your past decisions have been wrong or flawed?

- Have you any prejudices?
- Do you wish to block another's progress?
- Do you wish to impress?
- Are you trying not to offend someone?
- Would it have been uncomfortable to have gone another way and if so why?
- Remember the comfort zone.
- What role were you playing in the situation?

- ☐ How did you see those around you?
- ☐ Were you superior or inferior?
- ☐ Were you a leader or led?
- ☐ How did the others around you see you?
- ☐ What were their likes and dislikes?

Remember, in all this you must be totally honest with yourself. You must be painfully honest with yourself. This takes time to come to terms with.

You will not be able to move forward until you can honestly answer all these questions.

* * *

These fundamental issues are the spices in the stew of thinking. If they are right, then all the other ingredients will taste wonderful. You will cook a masterpiece. But if they are wrong, then the best ingredients in the world will be ruined.

The analogy of making a stew is very useful in discussing decision-making. Firstly, you must clearly understand the purpose for making it, who it is for and what are their requirements.

Small 'problems' require simple solutions. It causes stress not to make decisions. Do not put off such issues. Decide and clear your mind. The following discussion is about major issues requiring decision.

Then the issue for decision must be analysed and a plan drawn up based on all the information available.

Write it down in all its complexity. What information do you need to address each element of the task? This will give you your recipe for your stew.

You must collect all the necessary information from wherever it may be stored. You must get the best information possible, the best ingredients.

The next stage is the most important. Even if you have the best ingredients unless you cook in the right way you will fail.

Having got your information you should sort it and chop it up. Write it all down and lay it out in order. Then start to mix.

It is always essential to read over and ponder on all the information and leave it in the subconscious for a while to marinate.

As you read the information you should ask yourself how the pieces go together. Ask yourself questions, such as what would I do in this situation if it was happening to my mother or my wife or my child? What would I do if it was happening to me? What are the possible good outcomes of this situation? Could it go bad? List out all the pros and cons.

If there was a bad outcome how could you face it? You should develop a strategy for the difficult outcome to your deliberations.

The information needs to be looked at in many different ways. Have a look in a light-hearted way, a humorous way, particularly if others are involved.

The brain likes humour and a humorous approach relaxes the concentration.

Humour makes it possible to put unrelated things together in unusual ways, but out of this exercise may come the combinations that produce the perfect flavour. Humour will also help the subconscious functioning in the day-dream scenario.

Some elements in the cooking may need intense heat to bring out the flavour. So a period of absolute concentration is called for. Intense concentration is as useful as meditation or subconscious action at times. This is the back-to-the-wall scenario when all the faculties are focused absolutely on the project in hand. Virtuoso thinking.

But you must not overcook something, you may need a slow oven and no stirring. This is simply done by leaving all the information in the subconscious and carrying on with other tasks. Sleep on it.

SOME EXAMPLES

Let us take these various stages of thinking and see different examples. If you were to buy a car or a truck for your business this does not require emotion just hard-nosed business consideration. You would collect all of the necessary information. You would study that information carefully. And you would make a decision. Just concentrated thinking alone.

Most people decide to marry, for example, purely on a whim on instinct. They know very early on in a relationship about how they feel. They do not work out the cost of a wife, how much she will eat or whether or not she will be a good cook. There is no concentrated thinking. It is a purely an emotional decision. A product of the subconscious.

If you go to a restaurant you choose from a menu not by concentrated thought but directly from the subconscious, you know what you like and today you are in the mood for certain things, you will choose easily.

If you were a composer you could write a piece of music using all different forms of thought. A piece of music may be written purely, instinctively, straight from the subconscious; this, perhaps, would be the best music. However, it may be a job, a commission. Now it needs planning just like decision-making does.

Or it may be carried out with a great deal of difficulty. Forced onto the paper because it will not flow. This is purely concentrated thought.

In the final stage of cooking add seasoning to suit. The recipient certainly will.

You must take into account who will be affected. Will your decision affect other people? If it does, the others, or the other individual would have his own set of inadequacies with which to season your cooking. You must understand his perceptions.

Having finished preparing the meal it must be presented in the best possible way. It will be garnished to make it attractive. Presentation does not alter flavour but many would argue that it does.

In cooking you can tell how long a meal will take to prepare. A decision cannot be timed. You cannot force a decision. It will, however, become more predictable as long as the mind is understood and treated properly.

The answer always comes from within and nearly always after a period of relaxation. That relaxation may be meditation or sleep or solitude, or exercise.

Every time I write a speech I set a plan. Why am I giving it? Who or what is it about? I jot down notes on what I will say. I will read over some of my joke books. I will think over it while I run. Suddenly, after a week or so, an acceptable formula will become clear to me.

I believe that the only way to deal with these situations is to write all the information down. Only very brief notes are necessary. Then read and re-read perhaps re-write and re-structure, lay all the ingredients out in a new order.

PROBLEM-SOLVING

Not everything you need to make a decision about will be a problem. But every problem needs to be dealt with in a very similar way.

- Write the problem down. Analyse it. Who is involved? What is involved? Why does it exist? What are the possible outcomes, best or worst?
- How are you 'seasoning' the problem? Are you (because you are you) misreading the situation or misinterpreting it?
- On many occasions, having written down and analyzed the problem on paper, you can see that you are a big component in the problem. You have made it worse by your interpretation.

- As if you could reverse the process of making the stew, check the equipment i.e. your frame of mind. Check how you have seasoned it. Work out how the ingredients went together. Try to find out what went wrong. Are there too many ingredients? Are there too few ingredients?
- List all the possible causes of failure and all the possible solutions to them. Study all the options. Sleep on it.
- If there is an easy solution it will come or the best options will appear and then they can be given further analysis.
- Many people hold brain-storming sessions to accumulate as many possible options in any given situation as possible.
- For a brain-storming session a group of people will sit around a table and write out every thought they have on a particular subject without making any judgement or analysis during that meeting.
- The suggestions may be humorous or ridiculous, they may be factual or questioning. The mind will be encouraged to wander in every direction around a problem so that it is seen from every point of view.
- It is essential during these sessions to write down all possible options because otherwise the mind will become clogged with information and the subconscious will not get a chance to work.
- When you awaken in the middle of the night with any new thoughts write them down immediately. Keep the mind clear.

> *You need to stop thinking in order to relax before you make a decision.*
> - Any problem that you have will diminish in your perception of it and your subconscious will deliver a solution.

◇

95 | On guilt and blame

There is absolutely no benefit to you in indulging in guilt or blame. Both of these emotions concern situations that have already occurred. Why occupy your self-talk and therefore your whole body in blaming another? If you had a problem with a special friend you would go to him or her and talk about the problem and then you would agree to forget about it. Why should those about whom you care less occupy more of your time than those you like or love? The answer is obvious. Forgive these people in your own mind. You may even choose to go and talk to them and say that you forgive what has been done and then get on with the rest of your life.

No matter how long you spend feeling guilty about something that has happened you cannot change it, so the answer is simple: accept responsibility even if it is only in your own mind and get on with the rest of your life.

Worry, guilt, blame can occupy your self-talk and therefore it is easy to take control of the self-talk to eliminate these conditions.

However, it is possible to feel intense anxiety, tension or stress without being able to identify the particular situation which is causing it. At these times a deeper level of the subconscious is causing the discomfort.

* * *

I once had to arrange a four-day conference that involved a hundred people in organizing it and several years of preparation. The venue was going to cater for up to 10,000 people.

The opening ceremony was just two hours away and was to take place on the stage in the main tent. The floor of the tent was constructed to British Standard specifications. The stage was designed by specialists. On this tons of lighting equipment was erected and then over 30 tons of sound equipment was loaded.

During the final rehearsals the stage started to move. I was summoned and arrived into a discussion taking place between all interested parties as to who was to blame for the error. The discussion was going round in circles and getting nowhere, each arguing that his part in the construction was sound and everyone else was wrong.

The simple philosophy from the beginning was that we will never have problems – only challenges. There is no future in blame. The solution was in what we have discussed under problem-solving in section [20].

What exactly is the problem? What do we need to fix it? Who do we need to fix it? Where can we get them?

Within minutes people were sent to get material. Carpenters were summoned. At the same time, the stage was being dismantled to allow access for reinforcement.

While the champagne reception took place in another area, unknown to any of the invited guests, a crisis was resolved. Nobody knew until the next day.

There is never any future in blame yet our news programmes, our politics insist on finding who is to blame.

Lives are destroyed in the search for and in the attempt to apportion blame. A murderer or a thief or a drunken driver must be brought to justice for the safety of all. But finding a murderer and seeing him executed will never bring back a loved one.

96 On responsibility

Just recently, I read an extract from an article by a Japanese author comparing the USA with his own country. He had visited the Niagara Falls and was stunned by the lack of notices warning people away from danger, and the lack of fencing to protect people from falling over.

In Japan, there are rules and signs and fences to protect people from such circumstances. People expect others to be responsible for them, to protect them, by laws and then to be blamed if anything goes wrong.

Many people pay no regard to their own health and yet blame the doctor who does not save them.

We have a word in our language: 'accident'; this word implies no blame. Yet in every road accident blame must be apportioned. So the unpleasant occurrence will be perpetuated in the minds of those touched by the event.

A true accident cannot happen because there must be some element of carelessness, at least in most cases.

But since few of us are perfect what is the point in blame, and in trying to justify one's stance when all parties to the incident will be doing the same thing?

We can all think of people whose lives have been ruined by seeking to apportion blame or because of refusing to forgive others or accept responsibility for something.

We all know of those who refuse to enter new relationships because of a bad experience in the past which they will tell you about each time you meet them, showing how this earlier experience consumes their existence.

The solution is in honesty – honesty with oneself. Deep down, ask yourself: 'Did I contribute in any way to this situation?' This is not guilt, but accepting responsibility for one's actions. If the answer is yes then privately and deep down one must accept responsibility.

If you find this very difficult then you can see how the other party is feeling. Therefore, there can never be a solution. Or can there? There can be a solution in your own mind without telling anyone. Say to yourself and believe it: 'I can accept this situation because I contributed in some way to it.' Then leave it behind and move on.

97 On dealing with worry

Worry must be controlled; it cannot be allowed to control our self-talk and physiology. Here is the commonest suggested solution:

Take two pieces of paper. Write down exactly what the worry situation is.

On one piece of paper list everything you think can go wrong. On the other go through the list and write down what you can do to change that particular possible outcome. Having done this, write out in order of priority, the solutions that you see to each aspect of the worry situation. Decide what to do and do it. If it is night-time there is no further need to dwell on the worry situation until the morning.

You will often find that, having gone through this exercise, the situation seems much simpler. This exercise is also very useful for insomnia.

98 On the forces within and without

At this point it is worthwhile taking into account some of the other forces acting on our bodies which influence our existence and our state of mind. Accuracy in detail is not important with regard to what is being said here.

If we need to be aware of the forces controlling us from within and to be able to control them, it makes very good sense that we should be equally aware of all the other forces acting on us from without:

- We go through life without the need to be aware that we are constantly being sucked into the ground by the force of gravity and are enabled to walk only by the centrifugal force of the earth spinning at 1000 mph. The earth is also speeding through space in its journey around the sun and the whole galaxy is moving.
- We are subjected to 100 lbs/sq.in. of the atmosphere pressing down on us.
- The heat of the sun permits our existence.
- We live by the chemicals we take from the earth and the collection of gases from it that we breath.

99 How the body is affected chemically by our surroundings

This section draws together material that appears in many other parts of the book.

Our bodies are chemical machines receiving the supply of chemicals from many sources. Firstly, there are the obvious supplies:

- ☐ Food which supplies the chemicals required for existence, but also included are the many materials which interfere with the body, some causing profound allergic reactions, some causing only minor itching, some causing depression.
- ☐ Drink, giving a similar set of benefits and drawbacks.
- ☐ Medications.
- ☐ Inhaled gases with its own set of benefits and disadvantages.

The next supply of chemicals is through stimulation of the senses. Smells and sounds are immensely important triggers in instinctive reactions and in provoking memories.

- ☐ Smell – acting on the nostrils, triggering memories.
- ☐ Sound – with similar effects.
- ☐ Touch – perhaps the most significant early stimuli.
- ☐ Sight – with the effects of light and colour.
- ☐ Darkness – deprivation of stimuli leads to depression and fear.
- ☐ Sunlight – can cause vitamin D to be

produced in the skin, this is just one example. It can also burn and tan. It also causes feelings of happiness and elation.
- [ ] Wind – rain – cold – heat – Do these cause similar chemical release?
- [ ] The presence of other people. This is born out by research of the actions of people in waiting-rooms, among many other studies.
- [ ] The presence of physical obstructions. For example, an oppressive room.
- [ ] Atmospheric pressures. Mentioned earlier.

◇

100 On awareness

It is essential that we are aware of our surroundings and stimulations so that we know what is causing us to feel the way we do.

You need to develop your awareness to control the stimuli. Stop and look at a flower, see its beauty – its colour – its smell – its feel – how it glows in the light – how the rain lays on it – how it fits into its surroundings. Spend time looking at all things around you, see how they change every day.

As you enjoy, the positive effects will flow through your body. You need to be aware that all of those things about you that stimulate your senses in any way, have direct chemical effect on the body and that imput will evoke memories good or bad. See, be aware, and understand the imput. Understand your reaction. Control your reactions through your awareness.

All of these external chemicals act at two levels. Firstly, we can be aware and have conscious reactions. Secondly, they can precipitate pre-recorded responses in the subconscious – good or bad, happy or sad and cause mood changes according to the memories evoked.

Memories are chemical packages, storing emotional responses to a 'basket' of imput from a particular experience.

For example, memories of a wedding day. The 'basket' (collection) of stimuli would be: You are just outside the church. What was the light like? What were the clouds like? What were the smells in the air? What music did you hear? What time of the year was it? Were the birds singing? Were there bells ringing? The feel and smell of the clothes you were wearing, and many other items all going together to give that pleasant aura that comes with a memory of the moment.

101 On body rhythms and control

The body's control is to a large extent in its recorded daily rhythm. This is an on-going variety of chemical releases to control routines. These routines will be from waking through meal-times to sleeping and all the major functions of the day. Below these major events are the lesser functions like driving to work or starting work, your first coffee break etc. These functions down to the most minor part of your daily routines are controlled by chemical releases.

Similarly weekly, monthly, seasonal and annual, some say even seven-yearly cycles are controlled by chemical release right through our life.

Every second of every day is controlled in this way. If you decide to do any action your body immediately releases chemicals to enable you to do so, from answering the phone to eating a snack.

Stop and think of a lemon. A tangy, juicy shiny lemon with the skin still on which squirts from its pores a zing and juice as you bite into it.

Your mouth is watering.

When you go to do any job your body instantly prepares you for it. You can take conscious control over this or else your subconscious will take control for you or against you. It is possible to train for athletic events in your mind through intention.

This is why you do not need to try to change as mentioned earlier. *You do not need to put in effort to begin with because simply by a deep intention to do something your body is called on to produce the necessary chemistry to make it happen.*

This is why if you can clearly visualize in a crystal-clear picture what you wish to do and can be in that picture yourself, it must become a reality. The body will be so prepared and the chemicals released will be so potent that eventually the effort has to burst out of you, in the same way that unresolved stress must be released or it will destroy you.

Intention and visualization produce positive stress.

If your thinking is positive you will produce positive reactions. If your thinking is negative you will produce negative reactions or emotions. Emotions, as we know, are what you feel as a result of chemical releases from the brain.

Uncontrolled thought can be poisonous to the body.

You know that you can control your thoughts. Everyone else can as well. All I had to do is describe a lemon and your mouth watered. I can control your thoughts if you let me. Your subconscious also controls your thoughts. So you must take control, eliminate the bad routines. Understand all subconscious activity and be aware of the sources of outside control.

If the body renews itself almost entirely in a year, many parts in a week, it would seem to make sense to ensure that this renewal takes place in the best, most favourable and most positive chemical environment. This is in your control.

Remember 75% of all illness is psychogenic.

102 How to find happiness

Each time we sow a seed or plant a seedling we anticipate a luscious fast-growing plant which in most cases will bear a beautiful flower and/or bountiful succulent fruit. We expect a tree to grow majestically in beautiful form and to live to a very old age. Yet we all have in our houses and gardens plants that never achieve their potential.

You could, of course, buy some flowers and expertly place them on your ailing plant so that it looked natural. It would never look perfectly healthy against an unhealthy background, and it would certainly not bring forth fruit. It will wither and die and look silly.

The only way to make your unhealthy plant produce fruit would be to place it in the correct-sized pot with the best soil and to regularly fertilize it and water it. You must also keep it in the best light.

If you did not know what to do you would buy an appropriate book, or you would seek some expert help. Having treated your plant in the proper way it would, after a very short time be vibrant green and healthy and produce beautiful flowers in abundance.

Health of the plant and beautiful flowers come from within and not by dressing the sick plant with artificial flowers. Similarly, happiness and health come from within. Do you care for yourself as you would a favourite plant?

- ☐ Feed on the right things for body and mind.
- ☐ Be in the right environment.
- ☐ Seek help and guidance when necessary.
- ☐ Clear out the 'dead wood' from your mind.

Do these things and you will find lasting happiness. Happiness cannot be borrowed in any way that will enable it to last.

I have tried throughout this book to describe a deep understanding of self and good feelings towards others, and avoided using esoteric or religious language.

Many people can never experience satisfaction and cannot enjoy solitude because there are burdened by worry, guilt, anger, blame, and many other such restraints on their mind. These emotions clog up their mind so they constantly seek distractions from this turmoil.

You cannot achieve anything in life until you are at peace with yourself. Happiness comes with that peace. This book, therefore, is designed to allow you to enjoy your own company. It is designed to give you the freedom of your own mind. This is the only real freedom. This freedom can never be taken from you.

103 Travelling through life with conviction

Just to tease you into exploring the power of your own mind, here is little exercise which is taken from Brian Tracey's *Psychology of Achievement*.

Before you go on a journey, to the shops or the theatre, close your eyes and form a clear mental picture of the building you are going to. Get as sharp a picture as you can. Picture the doors, the windows, the pavement outside; see the people walking by and now picture a parking place. It will be there when you arrive.

As you make your journey, revisit the picture and believe firmly that the empty parking space will be there. It will be there. Travel each journey of your life with the same clarity of vision and belief in yourself.

It sounds a little silly doesn't it? You do not have to tell anyone just try it. As I have said before, people cannot share some of these deep beliefs with you. They are personal.

My family and I use this visualization all the time – and not just for parking. Even my youngest child believes in the power of visualization.

I use it successfully all the time. We recently went three times to a local theatre. I, to the annoyance of the other occupants of the car, insisted on driving into the car-park even though there was a continuous stream of cars leaving, having given up the search for parking.

Each time I found a single parking space. Each time was nearer to the entrance. Travel with conviction in your life.

104 Twelve ways to improve the function of the mind

1) A medical check up. It is amazing how many slight deficiencies the body can slow down function of body and mind.
2) Physical exercise. Keep fit. A minimum of 30 minutes aerobic exercise three times a week.
3) Solitude. It is essential to have a period of solitude each day. This period of solitude should be used by refusing to let any thought occupy your mind. Chase all the thoughts away. Let the mind wander.
4) Listen to relaxing music. Explore the classics for suitable music.
5) Read suitable material. Start and finish the day by reading small excerpts from philosophy.
6) Humour. Always try to find occasions to laugh during the day. Read humour.
7) Exercise the mind by doing puzzles, crosswords and problem-solving.
8) Eat well. Eat healthy foods.
9) Limit your intake of alcohol. Alcohol obviously interferes with the functioning of the mind in the short term, and continuous use interferes with its functioning in the long term, although not irreparably.
10) Use positive thinking at all times. Remember the key words are motivation and visualization.
11) Improve your awareness and thereby

enhance the benefits to you from all your senses.
12) Understand the benefits of *intention* and use it to build the chemistry of success.

◇

105 The end and the beginning

Your body is a machine which has a capacity to be controlled in many ways.

- [ ] It can be controlled by default, which will keep it alive while asleep or unconscious. This is the autonomic nervous system.
- [ ] While awake one can function without any conscious control; zombie-like; yet, for example, walk or drive safely.

This is carried out by the autonomic nervous system and the subconscious.

To enable the subconscious control of the body in default, the body 'learns' from each new experience and logs it in the memory so that similar experiences will be dealt with in a similar way when encountered in the future.

- [ ] You can also be controlled by external imput playing on your subconscious, by body language, by sound, by speech, by light and by the environment.
- [ ] You can also be manipulated in all of these areas by someone wishing to control you for whatever reason, sinister or otherwise.
- [ ] You can be hypnotized.
- [ ] You can be controlled by food or drink, by

drugs or medication, either intentionally or by accident and of course intentionally by others.

* * *

YOU CAN TAKE CONTROL of every area of your life.

- [ ] You can take control of the circadian rhythms. To have rhythm and routine in your life.
- [ ] The fuel supply for the body machine – the chemical machine – is in the chemicals put into the body. You can take control of this.
- [ ] All outside influences on you can be controlled.
- [ ] You can be aware of the ability of others to manipulate you even if they do not know that they are manipulating you.
- [ ] You can choose to live and work in a relaxed environment also. You can control colour – sound – smell – light – space – tidiness around you – etc.
- [ ] You can take control of, and improve the functional ability of the body by:

  - Exercise
  - Solitude
  - Relaxation
  - Meditation

- [ ] You can improve imput by awareness and thus sharpen the senses.
- [ ] Those who have taken control of their

- [ ] body to the extreme can control heart rate and blood pressure and all other areas of the body.
- [ ] Since 75% of illness is psychogenic you can to a very large extent take control of the risks to your body from illness.
- [ ] You can call up the necessary chemistry in your body by:

  - Intention of any action
  - Visualization, to get it right
  - Motivation to give you energy
  - Humour to relax the mind

But before you can do all of this you must know yourself. Know what the incorrect default instructions are. Then you can change.

You do this by:

- [ ] Regression into your past and examining your reactions
- [ ] By recording your dreams, studying them and analysing your reactions
- [ ] By recording what causes you to be stressed
- [ ] By recording what causes you to be depressed.

You can learn to deal with your negative emotions like:

- Worry
- Guilt
- Fear
- Anger

You alter these faults by replacing them in your mind with new ones through repetition and through thought.

You must take total responsibility for your life. There is no room for blame.

You must learn not to make judgements. Remember that you teach people to treat you the way you do.

WHEN YOU HAVE DONE THIS YOU WILL FIND PEACE OF MIND AND THEREFORE THE BASIS FOR SUCCESS

YOU HAVE ALREADY STARTED TO LIVE YOUR LIFE OVER.

IF YOU SEEK TO CHANGE and you know who the real you is; if you can see the logic of all that has been said and accept all that is untrue in your mind; if you can see how this effects your thinking and therefore your judgement – you have taken a major step forward.